TREASURE HIDDEN IN DARKNESS

WHEN THE WAYS OF GOD
PRODUCE THE ACTS OF GOD

JIM NEWSOM

Treasure Hidden in Darkness
by Jim Newsom
Copyright ©2021 Jim Newsom

ISBN 978-1-63360-182-6

Unless otherwise identified, Scripture quotations are taken from The Holy Bible: New International Version ©1978 by the New York International Bible Society, used by permission of Zondervan Bible Publishers. All rights reserved.

Scripture quotations marked GNT are taken from the Good News Translation* (Today's English Version, Second Edition). Copyright © 1992 American Bible Society. All rights reserved.

Scripture quotations marked ESV are taken from the English Standard Version, Copyright © 2001 by Crossway, a publishing ministry of Good News Publishers.

Scripture quotations marked NET are taken from the New English Translation, (NET Bible*) copyright ©1996-2017 by Biblical Studies Press.

Scripture quotations marked TLB are taken from The Living Bible, copyright © 1971 by Tyndale House Foundation.

Scripture quotations marked NKJV are taken from the New King James Version*. Copyright © 1982 by Thomas Nelson. Used by permission. All rights reserved

Scripture quotations marked MSG are taken from The Message, copyright © 1993, 2002, 2018 by Eugene H. Peterson. Used by permission of NavPress. All rights reserved. Represented by Tyndale House Publishers, Inc.

Scripture quotations marked BSB are taken from the Berean Study Bible, Copyright ©2016, 2020 by Bible Hub, used by Permission.

Scripture quotations marked KJV are taken from the King James Version and rest in the public domain.

Scripture quotations marked NASB are taken from the Holy Bible, New American Standard Bible, copyright © 1960, 1971, 1977, 1995, 2020 by The Lockman Foundation. All rights reserved.

Scripture quotations marked ASV are taken from the American Standard Version and rest in the public domain.

Scripture quotations marked AAT are taken from The Bible: An American Translation, copyright © 1931, The University of Chicago Press. All rights reserved.

For Worldwide Distribution   Printed in the U.S.A.

Urban Press
P.O. Box 8881
Pittsburgh, PA 15221-0881
412.646.2780
www.urbanpress.us

TABLE OF CONTENTS

Foreword by Charles Simpson
vii

Introduction
ix

CHAPTER ONE
You Don't Have to Die for the Pain to Stop
(God's way of bringing salvation to my sin-sick soul)
1

CHAPTER TWO
Bad Days Are Good Days in Disguise
(God's way of working together the bad that happens to us to produce His good for us)
14

CHAPTER THREE
A Flowing River Is Self-Purifying
(God's way of using mission to others to produce maintenance for ourselves)
28

CHAPTER FOUR
Who Has Your Lunch?
(God's way of sustaining you is when you bring sustenance to others)
34

CHAPTER FIVE
God Doesn't See the Trash in Our Lives but the Treasure in Our Souls
(God's way of bringing the message to the worthless and then using the worthless to bring the message)
42

CHAPTER SIX
God Will Fix a Fix to Fix You
(God's way of taking the worst of times and using them to produce the best of times)
52

CHAPTER SEVEN
What to Do When Your Past Begins to Chase You
(God's way of using what is in our future to produce ministry for our past)
62

CHAPTER EIGHT
Thorns That Help
(God's way of using our weakness to produce His strength)
77

CHAPTER NINE
**Desiring God's Judgments
Instead of Dreading Them**
(God's way of using His judgment of our lives to produce His
righteousness in our lives)
89

CHAPTER TEN
Getting A Bigger Frying Pan
(God's way of leading us through something earthy in order
help us hear something heavenly)
102

CHAPTER ELEVEN
The Breeze Is Worth The Flies
(God's way of using how we receive His minister to determine
how much of His ministry is released)
115

CHAPTER TWELVE
**Dry Times Are for Promotion
not Punishment**
(God's way of taking that which stimulates thirst to
produce a pool that satisfies thirst)
127

CHAPTER THIRTEEN
**A Dent in Your Armor Doesn't
Disqualify You For The Battle**
(God's way of using our failures to produce His successes)
139

CHAPTER FOURTEEN
Forced to Trust God Totally
(God's way of using the sickness of my body to
bring healing to my soul)
152

**About Jim Newsom
Contact Information**

FOREWORD

Jim Newsom is a gifted speaker and teacher who has already touched thousands of lives. As you read this book, you will realize that he is also a gifted writer. I have known Jim for more than 36 years and have recommended his ministry on many occasions. He is one of my favorite speakers.

It is not often that we find a story like this one: a life taker becomes a life giver. Having known the author for many years, I cannot imagine the person that he was. His story is one of amazing grace—a new creation. There is no effort to excuse or "gloss over" the person he was., and the person he has become will be evident to the reader.

The message of this book is very close to my own heart:"Good things are found in bad places." Jim fortifies the message with biblical theology, examples, humor, and personal experience. Jim is a treasure that was found in darkness.

Our daughter and son-in-law minister to children in Latin America. They work with children and mothers in the most dire of circumstances. The ministry is called, "Hidden Treasures." Five of those children are now our legally adopted grandchildren. You can understand why the substance of this book is close to my own heart.

The theology and philosophy presented by *Treasure Hidden In Darkness* are the foundation for every redemptive endeavor, including the mission of Jesus to earth. He found "jewels" in the darkened world (see Malachi 3:17). That is the heart of God.

Sometimes great truth is obscured by difficult language or tedious style. One author asked a friend, "Have you read my last book?" The friend replied, "I hope so." That will not be the case here. Jim has developed the ability to turn a phrase by his years of speaking. His style is well crafted and clean. The phrases penetrate with truth. In some cases, I thought of his phrases like a jackhammer breaking up one's hardened attitude toward those who still reside in dark places. Though the message is indeed serious, it is often laced with humor. The author is at ease with himself and the reader.

Most of us who labor in and love the Church realize that the Church must break out of itself. In many cases, religion has become a prison of routine and isolation. Building bigger and better churches must give way to becoming "treasure hunters" and "pearl merchants." This book will inspire that change of focus.

Jim is the result of someone who believed that treasures can be found in dark places. He came to understand that truth through his own experience and now he gives us both the message and the model. His life is a prophesy to us of what must happen as we turn outward. There are more Jim Newsom's out there—many more. The Lord is calling us to see them in a new way. This book will help us to see their treasures in their darkness.

Charles Simpson
Mobile, Alabama

INTRODUCTION

As you will read in the first chapter of this book, I spent the first eight years of my Christian life in a Florida prison. It was there in prison that I began to read the Bible. One of the first Scriptures God quickened to my heart and opened my mind to understand was Psalm 103:7. This verse makes two statements, the first about an individual, Moses, and the second about a nation of people, Israel. The statement about Moses was "God made known His ways" to him. The statement to the nation of Israel was "God made known His acts" to them.

What initially caught my attention was the statement made about Israel. Having read the Book of Exodus, I noticed the word *acts*, defined as God's supernatural power to deliver out of bondages and to provide guidance, resources, and power. Two other versions of the Bible render that part of the verse this way: "He caused the people of Israel to see his mighty deeds" (TEV) and "He showed all Israel what He could do" (CEV). At the time I read this, I was in desperate need of God's supernatural power to deliver, make provision, and display might. Like Israel, I wanted God to show me what He could do on my behalf and let me see His mighty acts.

What was really encouraging to me about this particular part of the verse was that it was the nation of Israel He was talking about. Again, because I had already read the book of Exodus, I knew what kind of people were in the nation of Israel. They were at their best an imperfect people and at their worst a rebellious people. The writer of Exodus used words like *stiff-necked, stubborn,* and *complainers* to describe them. The reason I found this encouraging was because those words described me. Therefore, if God would make known His acts to them despite how they were, then He would have no problem making known His acts to me as well.

Because I was in such need, I started praying this verse every day, "Lord like You did for the nation of Israel, please make known Your acts to me as well." I prayed it daily for several weeks with no tangible results. In my frustration, I decided to re-read the verse. This time, I sensed the Lord wanted me to meditate on the statement that was made about Moses. As I did, the Spirit showed me that Moses was the catalyst God used to make known His acts to Israel. Because Moses knew God's ways, the children of Israel saw God's acts. It was then I began to understand the concept that "the ways of God produce the acts of God." Therefore, if I wanted to see God's acts demonstrated in and through my life, then it was imperative I learn His ways.

However, there is a problem knowing His ways, and that is they are beyond knowing. Isaiah 55:8-9 states, "For my thoughts are not your thoughts, neither are your ways my ways, declares the LORD. For as the heavens are higher than the earth, so are my ways higher than your ways and my thoughts than your thoughts" (ESV). "As high as the heaven is above the earth" is the distance between the way God does things and the way we do things. That's why in Psalm 103:7 the psalmist wrote "that God made know His ways to Moses" because only God can bridge that gap. There is nothing I can do to make this happen because what I need to see is invisible; what I need to hear is inaudible; and what I need to know surpasses knowledge. My only hope was that He would make known His ways to me as He did to Moses and would also inject Himself into the equation and open up my finite mind so I could grasp the infinite wonders of His ways.

Proverbs 25:2 states, "It is the glory of God to conceal a matter, but the glory of kings is to search out a matter" (NAS). God loves to hide who He is and what He has in places where we don't normally look. Isaiah 45:3 states, "I will give you treasures hidden in dark vaults" (NEB). The Hebrew word translated *treasures* is *owtsar* and is defined as a *treasure house*. The Hebrew word translated *darkness* is *choshek* and is defined as *the darknesses of misery, destruction, ignorance, death, and wickedness*. The word *darkness* describes the condition of the container and the word *treasure* describes the value of the contents. The implication of this verse is that God hides some of our greatest treasures in the darkest circumstances and situations of our lives.

This book is a result of discovering some of God's greatest treasures (His acts) in the midst of some of the darkest times (His ways) of my life. It was in the midst of the darkness of dying to something that interested me that I discovered the treasure of coming alive to that which interests God. It was in the midst of the darkness of my loss that I discovered the treasure of His gain. It was in the midst of the darkness of my failure that I discovered the treasure of His success. And it was in the midst of the darkness of always being last where the world was concerned that I discovered the treasure of always being first where He was concerned. Please join me in learning God's ways by sifting through the dark times in your life so you can also begin to see His acts demonstrated, thereby getting in on all the treasures He has for you.

Jim Newsom
Jeffersonville, Indiana
December 2021

ONE

YOU DON'T HAVE TO DIE FOR THE PAIN TO STOP

God's way of bringing salvation to my sin-sick soul

Let me start by sharing some of my past so you can understand the things that led up to my conversion to Christ. I would like to preface all my statements about my past with this statement: I am utterly embarrassed and ashamed of the direction my life took when I was 14 years old. I wasn't ashamed of it then. If anything, I was rather proud and arrogant about it. I have had a lot of years to think about how my earlier years contributed to my overall demise as well as the demise of others. In my pursuit of good times, good feelings, notoriety, and fast money, I damaged a lot of people in my wake as I raced through life. Some of those people have been damaged irreparably and are suffering today and will suffer all the days of their lives because they had the misfortune of running into me during their lifetime.

Where I have been able to make amends, I have. Where I have been able to make restitution, I have. If I knew how to do any more, I would. Like a lot of things in life, however, no matter how badly you would like to undo them, you can't. It's like ringing a bell, for once it has been rung, you can never un-ring it. At that point, you can only do two things. One is to learn to live with it, and by the mercy and grace of God, I have been able to do that. Then you try to redeem it by allowing God to bring something good out of something so bad. This book, especially this first chapter, is an attempt to redeem my past by telling my story, hopefully preventing someone from making the mistakes I did.

At first, I didn't know if God could or would do that in my situation. I knew He redeemed me from my past, but I wasn't sure He could use my past to bring redemption to others. But over the years, in schools, prisons, and churches, I have seen Him to do just that. It's my prayer He will do it for you wherever it needs done as I share my past.

FAILING AT LIFE

I was born on August 15, 1950, in the city of Pittsburgh, Pennsylvania into a lower middle-class family. My father loaded trucks for the Sears & Roebuck Company and my mother was an office worker. I have three brothers—one who is two years older, one who is one year older, and one who is two years younger than I. Though we always had enough to eat, clothes to wear, and a roof over our heads, we didn't have much else.

My parents were not Christians and therefore we never went to church. As a result, I grew up completely ignorant of spiritual matters. Though they were not Christians, they were moral, hard-working people who wanted the best for their children. My mother instilled in me a love for academics. She told me if I excelled in academics, I could write my own ticket in life. My father instilled in me a love for athletics. He also told me if I excelled in any given sport, I could write my own ticket in life. At an early age, I sought to excel in both areas, so much so that by the time I was a sophomore in high school, I was an honor roll student while excelling in basketball. I was also college bound and hoped to earn a scholarship to play basketball, going on to study and become a lawyer.

At the same time this was happening, society was going through some major upheavals. It was the mid-'60s and a lot of things were changing. President Kennedy had been assassinated, the Vietnam War was beginning, and the Civil Rights Movement was growing. Of all the changes that happened during that era, however, the one that affected me the most was the change in music. Rock 'n roll music went from an Elvis Presley style of an individual musician and singer to a Beatles style with a band. Like a lot of people of my time, I got caught up in this new style of music. Not only did I enjoy the music, I wanted to emulate the lifestyles of the musicians, which included both the abuse and use of drugs and alcohol.

At first, I used drugs and alcohol in moderation, but before long, they took over my life. By that I mean that getting high and having fun became my sole preoccupations in life. Everything took a back seat to these new passions in my life, and that included my family, education, and playing basketball. This caused my life, which was on an upward spiral, to begin a downward spiral, so much so that eight years later, I had failed at every aspect of life.

I failed as a son in that I broke my mother's heart to the extent that four years later, when she was diagnosed with cancer, she had no will to fight it and died a year later. It also took me 15 years to get my father to speak to me again after that. I don't judge him for his decision because he learned early on that the best way to deal with me was from a distance. Any time he allowed his fatherly compassion to kick in, and he did allow that to happen on several occasions, I would come in and wreak havoc, not only in his life, but also in the lives of my brothers. I failed as a sibling in that it took 18 years to get my brother who is two years older to speak to me; 19 years to get my brother who is one year older to speak to me; and more than 25 years to get my brother who is two years younger to speak to me.

I failed as a student in that I was expelled from high school in my senior year. What started out to be my first big victory in life ended up being my first big failure. I had already been suspended for minor infractions of school rules but one day in November of my senior year, I came to school a little hung over and in a bad mood. A particular teacher who took it upon himself to harass me on a daily basis did so one too many times, and I assaulted him. For that indiscretion, I was expelled. I thought this teacher harassed me because he didn't like me, I later found out, much too late, that he actually harassed me because he thought the world of me. He remembered how I was as a sophomore and freshman and thought maybe a strong stance would bring me back to the potential I had once shown.

My expulsion brought my parents to their wits' end. Not knowing what to do with me, they encouraged me to join the Army. They were hoping the Army would succeed where they felt they had failed, thinking the regimen and discipline of military life would bring me back to my senses and I could recapture the promise of my youth. Because I didn't think I had a problem, I proceeded to fail as a soldier, in that I went AWOL several times, received numerous Article 15s, one Battalion Article 15, one Summary Court Martial, one Special Court Martial, and was eventually undesirably discharged. From my warped perspective, I held my discharge up much like I had my expulsion, almost as a badge of honor. To me it signified that my parents couldn't break me, school officials couldn't break me, and now the army couldn't break me. What I didn't know was that I was breaking myself.

During this time, my drug and alcohol usage were steadily increasing. Since I didn't like to work, I turned to crime to pay for my addiction. As a result, I failed as a criminal in that I have been apprehended by the authorities on 30 different occasions, resulting in several arrests. Most of my arrests were for possession of drugs, sales of drugs, or criminal activity to get drugs. I have been arrested for robbing drug stores in South Carolina; arrested for possession of eight pounds of marijuana in Georgia; arrested for having two hundred tabs of LSD in Florida; and arrested for possession of heroin and heroin paraphernalia in Pennsylvania—just to name a few.

Finally, I made the ultimate failure in a moment that

I will never be able to get back, a moment that I will regret for the rest of my life. I failed as a human being in that I took somebody's life in a drug-related incident. Now if anyone would have ever told me when I was 14 and smoking my first joint that I would be responsible for taking somebody's life eight years later, I would have told them they were crazy. When I committed this crime, however, something snapped inside me that is hard to describe. I was surprised at how deeply I felt the guilt and torment of my actions for up until this time, I had become a case study of what a sociopath is in that I acted without a conscience.

I could bankrupt my own dad when I was a heroin addict—and did—and think nothing of it. I could allow my own little brother to go to jail for something that I did and feel nothing over it. But when I took someone's life, it was like all the remorse I should have been feeling all along came flooding in on me all at one time, and the pain that I was feeling was more than I could bear.

There is a Scripture that describes what I was going through, although I didn't know it then. I later discovered it as I read the Bible in Proverbs 28:17: "A man who is laden with the guilt of human blood will be a fugitive until death; let no one support him" (NAS). *The Living Bible* says it more clearly, "A murderer's conscience will drive him into hell. Don't stop him!"

FINDING THE LORD

During that fateful day, I tried all my crutches to numb me to this pain, but to no avail. I tried getting stoned, but all it did was amplify the pain. I tried getting drunk, but all that did was intensify the pain. Somewhere in the midst of these attempts, it dawned on me that the only way I was going to get relief from what I was feeling—and I was being driven to get relief—was if my life ended. I had never been suicidal before, but I longed for death, if death would stop this pain. At the time, I remember being struck by the sheer irony of my situation.

I initially did drugs to feel good, I was now doing them so I wouldn't feel so bad. I initially did drugs because they sharpened my senses, but now I was doing them in order to dull my senses. I initially did drugs to feel better about myself, but now because of them I hated myself to the point of suicide. And finally, I initially did drugs because I thought they would help me be the person I always wanted to be, but ultimately, they caused me to become what I hated most—a murderer.

Two other things contributed to my self-loathing. The first was the person I killed was someone I was close to. Nobody knew I was responsible, but I knew it and the knowledge of it was eating me alive. The second was that the wake was being held at my house, because my house was the only house big enough to accommodate the crowd. The only positive aspect of this for me was that during the wake, there would be a lot of drugs present. This knowledge helped me formulate the plan of my suicide. I decided that since I lived by drugs, I was going to die by drugs. Therefore, my plan was that during the wake, I would just keep ingesting drugs until I overdosed. But for some reason, God had a different plan for me.

It wasn't that I hit bottom and looked up; like always when I hit bottom, I wasn't looking for a way up, I was looking for a way out. However, in my looking for a way out, God went out of His way to provide a way up for me. Different people were calling me during the course of the day, saying they had heard about what happened, and could they come to the wake. One particular girl by the name of Lynn called and asked if she could come over, and I responded with a yes. The only reason I said yes was the fact that the last time I had seen her, which was about four months earlier, I had sold her a fairly large quantity of drugs. Thinking she was still in the same lifestyle, I said yes. Had I known she had become a Christian since the last time I had seen her, I would have never let her into my house.

A couple of hours later, Lynn arrived armed with a smile that wouldn't quit and an industrial-sized Bible. She came walking up to me and said, "Praise God." My initial thoughts were, "Great, just when I thought things couldn't get any worse, a Jesus Freak shows up at my door; I already feel terrible about myself, and she is going to just make me feel worse." In anger, I told my live-in girlfriend to take her inside to talk with her for a few minutes, then get rid of her. My girlfriend at that time was as hard and cold as I was, and I was confident she could get rid of her, even if she had to be rude and profane.

More than an hour later, however, and the two of them were still inside the house. In the meantime, several other people showed up for the wake, most of them being drug dealers like I was. I was keeping them outside until the "Jesus Freak" left. Sensing there must be a problem, I called in and asked my girlfriend to come out for a moment. When I asked her why she hadn't yet gotten rid of the Jesus Freak, she responded by telling me that Lynn refused to leave until she had a chance to talk to me because she said that God had sent her for that purpose.

At this point, I was angry and determined to get her out of my house. I told the people who had arrived what was happening and told them the best way to get her to leave would be to go inside and start taking the drugs that everyone had brought. I especially was anxious to get on with the plan that I had formulated earlier, for the sooner I could end my life and stop this pain the better. As we went into the house, I let about 14 others go first. Everybody avoided sitting next to the Jesus Freak so all the other seats were taken except the one right next to Lynn.

My pride wouldn't allow me sit on the floor since it was my house and I was not going to permit this girl to intimidate me. Sitting next to her was all the opportunity she needed to start preaching to me about God. She had that industrial-sized Bible in one hand and was pointing her finger at me with the other hand. All this did was anger me while also confirming my negative feelings about Christians. As she quoted Scripture verses to me, I responded with vulgar and profane language. For the next 20 minutes, I battled to get her out of my house and she battled to get something into my heart.

After these 20 minutes, she realized the approach she was taking was not working, so suddenly she stopped talking,

bowed her head, and began praying. After what seemed like
an hour, she lifted her head, and I could see she had been
crying. With as much compassion as I have ever seen in the
eyes of another person, she said to me, "Jim, you don't have
die for the pain to stop, somebody has already died for you
and His name is Jesus Christ." What struck me about those
comments was wondering how she knew. Nobody in that
room knew the pain I was in, and nobody knew I was contemplating suicide. Even though I didn't believe in God, the
only conclusion I could come to was that this God who had
sent her must have told her.

Suddenly it dawned on me that she was offering me
another solution other than suicide. This possibility caused
faith to enter my heart and moved me from hopelessness
to hope. My next comment to her was, "What do I have to
do?" She took my hand and led me out of the living room
into the dining room. I had to step over many of my friends
who were inquiring what I was doing, but I was completely
oblivious to them. My only concern was finding this God
who had spoken so kindly to me. In the dining room, Lynn
had me get down on my knees and then she simply led me
through the sinner's prayer. When I got to the part where I
repeated, "Jesus, forgive me of my sins, come into my heart,
and change my life," immediately the burden that was crushing my soul was lifted, and I was filled a joy and a peace that
I had never known. I began to cry, first for the wretchedness
of my sin, and then for the joy of my salvation. I immediately
jumped to my feet and turned to my friends to share with
them what had just happened to me.

I don't know what my friends saw when I prayed, but
whatever it was it spooked them. I saw them stumbling over
one another trying to get out the door. My best friend at
that time, Terry, was the last one out the door, and I yelled
to him "Terry where are you going?" He looked at me with
horror and said, "Jim, we'll come back when you're feeling
better." I yelled to him as he was going out the door, "I've
never felt better!"

Lynn stayed and talked with me for a little while, encouraging me to get a Bible and begin reading it. That night

when I went to bed, my mind was bombarded with thoughts like, "Do you really believe that a holy and just God could forgive you for all the things you've done to others?" Not knowing about spiritual warfare and that I now had an enemy of my soul who would love to see me lose what I had gained by faith, I didn't know how to combat what I was thinking. I did know that the sense of confidence I had earlier was beginning to wane. I had to do something, so I began to say over and over again, "I do believe in Jesus, I do believe in Jesus, I do believe in Jesus." As I did this, peace returned to my heart and I fell asleep.

FOLLOWING HIS LEADING

The next morning, I awakened at 7:00 a.m., which was the first miracle of my Christian life for it had been years since I had seen 7:00 a.m. unless I stayed up that late. I also awoke with a clear head and a hungry heart. I made a cup of coffee and sat on my back porch. The newness of life was overwhelming. As I sat there, the sky was bluer, the clouds were whiter, I could smell the fragrance of flowers, and I could hear the birds chirping in the background. I felt more alive at that moment than at any other time in my life. I thought to myself that it was as if I had been born again. According to the Bible, that is exactly what had happened to me, but I didn't realize that until later on when I began to read the Bible. The only terminology I knew at that time was, "I was saved."

As I was sitting there, reveling in my newfound life, a thought came into my mind, that I later discovered as I began to grow as a Christian was the still small voice of the Lord: "Son, if you surrendered your life to Me, you need to surrender your life to the authorities." Normally this would have been a foreign thought to someone like me. All my life, I made it an art form to escape anything difficult. When my home life got tough, I ran away; when school got tough, I cut class; when the army got tough, I went AWOL; and when life got tough, I smoke something, swallowed something, drank something, snorted something, or injected something—but I always managed to escape. On that back porch, however,

I was facing the most difficult decision of my life, and there was something in me that wanted to do the right thing. This thought not only told me what to do, it imparted the faith and peace I needed to be able to do it.

As a result, another person and I drove up to the sheriff's department for the purpose of turning ourselves in. As I entered the county sheriff's office, I approached an officer who I recognized sitting behind a counter and he recognized me. He looked surprised, because normally I didn't walk in the front door on my own, but was usually dragged through the side door against my will. As a result, he was immediately guarded and asked me what I was doing there. I told him that I was there to turn myself in for a crime I was responsible for committing. He didn't believe me and told me to sit in the lobby until he checked my story out. After waiting two hours, I was arrested.

I then confessed to the crime that I was responsible for. The other person I was with was arrested as well. We both were charged with involuntary manslaughter due to culpable negligence. Before I was able to plead guilty to that, I was told that I was now being charged with second degree murder. I didn't believe at the time that I was guilty of that, so I pled not guilty to that charge. During my trial, the prosecuting attorney while trying to convince the jury I was guilty, convinced me! What convinced me was the definition that he gave for second degree murder, which was someone of a depraved mind and has no regard for human life. Since I was that kind of a person, I changed my plea from not guilty to guilty.

Three weeks later, I stood before the judge for sentencing. I was confident the Lord was going to help me, that He was going to do good for me. At that time, I didn't realize that God doesn't use my definition of what is good because He has His own. At the time, I thought probation or the minimum sentence would be good for me, but the Lord didn't see it that way. After the judge came out and sat down, he looked at me and smiled. I mistook his smile for a sign that the Holy Spirit had softened his heart and thus was going to get a light sentence. In reality, he was smiling because he was about to give out a sentence he was going to enjoy giving. There I stood, a man expelled from high school, undesirably discharged from the army, with a record as long as my arm, who had pled guilty without making a deal. What that judge couldn't give to others because of legal restraints, he could finally give to me. He said to me, "Young man, I sentence you to the maximum sentence allowed by law and if I could give you more I would—30 years."

I wasn't prepared for this sentence because I was confident God was going to help me. After all, I surrendered my life to Him and then at His leading had surrendered to the authorities. I confessed, eventually pled guilty, and I even quit smoking three days before my sentencing to prove to God that I was worthy of any mercy He would bestow on my behalf. After all that, this is my reward? 30 years? I was angry, disappointed, and disillusioned.

On the van ride back to the county jail, I smoked five cigarettes at once out of spite. How could God allow this to happen? I did everything that I sensed He wanted me to do. I had a crisis of faith and had every intention of turning my back on the Lord. My plan was to go back to my cell, get my Bible, tear out the pages one at a time and flush them down the toilet. Before I could tear out the first page, however, I had another thought, much like the one that led me to turn myself in: "Dummy, now is not the time to throw the book with all the answers away. You're going to prison for 30 years and you're going to need this book now more than ever." This thought made sense to me and helped me settle down. I then decided I had already come too far with the Lord to turn back now. Even though I didn't know what my future held, I did know who held my future.

Though in the natural, this seemed like the worst thing that could happen to me, it was in fact one of the best things that had ever happened to me. Incarceration was one of God's ways to produce in me and for me many of His acts. For it was in the darkness of my prison sentence that I discovered many of the treasures I now impart to people all over the world.

My life is about all the great things that have happened

to me, in me, and through me since I made those two mo-
mentous decisions in July of 1972. The first was to surrender
my life to Christ and the second to surrender my life to the
authorities. Those two decisions helped me realize that you
can't put something behind you until you face it. Though
God forgave me of the sin of murder, I still had to face the
consequences of that sin. Therefore, as I faced those consequences with faith in God, He was able to do two things
through those consequences: He was able to minimize the
damage and maximize the good. I came to realize that God
allowed my 30-year sentence not to hurt or punish me, but
to help and train me. Therefore, today I see my sentence as
a provision or benefit of my salvation and not a penalty for
my sin.

In fact, let me go one step further. One of God's greatest expressions of love ever demonstrated to me was that
sentence. Had I received probation or a lighter sentence, I
would have gotten out of jail prior to my ability to handle
freedom in the midst of my newfound faith. I am convinced
the enemy would have exploited my weaknesses and I would
be dead today. As it was, after I was paroled eight years later, I
almost didn't make it. I then realized that part of God's provision of protection for me was prison. I now tell audiences
everywhere that I wasn't arrested but rescued.

After spending eight of my thirty-year sentence
in prison, they gave me the remainder on parole. I spent
ten years on parole and in 1990 my parole was terminat-
ed. When I got out of prison, I attended a two-year Bible
school of ministry in Gainesville, Florida. While I was going through the school, I became a youth pastor for the
church that sponsored the school. Two years later, in March
of 1982, I took an associate pastor position at another church
in Inverness, Florida. While there, I met and married my
wife, Diane. In September of 1983, Diane and I relocated
to Orlando, Florida, where I started Rivers of Living Water
Ministries. In 1986, I started Covenant Church of Orlando.
In 1992, my family and I relocated to Lancaster, Pennsylvania
to start a Northeast branch of Rivers of Living Water. While
in Lancaster, I helped plant Faith Covenant Church. Then in

August of 2003, my family and I relocated again, this time to Louisville, Kentucky, to start a new ministry called Outward Focused.

One of the best decisions I ever made when I first met the Lord was to follow His leadings. God is supernatural and He often intervenes in our lives through supernatural means. His interventions, however, are usually limited to leading us, protecting us, or supplying our needs. Proverbs 3:5-6 says, "Trust in the Lord with all thine heart and lean not unto thine own understanding. In all thy ways acknowledge Him, and He shall direct thy paths." When you fully commit a situation to God, He will take the initiative to fulfill His will in your life. Fully committing a situation to God does not ensure that you will know the solution; it just promises God will lead you. You may or may not be consciously aware of His leading. The next time you are faced with a decision, commit it to God. He may give you the wisdom to make the right choice. If He does not, you can still be assured God will successfully direct your life. Even if you make the wrong choice, God will still work all things together for your good (see Romans 8:28).

TWO

BAD DAYS ARE GOOD DAYS IN DISGUISE

God's way of working together the bad that happens to us to produce His good for us

Psalm 139:16 says, "You saw me before I was born and scheduled each day of my life before I began to breathe" (TLB). Think about that for a moment. Before you were even born, God scheduled each day you were going to live. Since God is doing the scheduling, then you know that each one of these days has the promise of good for your life. Psalm 118:24 further explains, "This is the day which the Lord has made let us rejoice and be glad in it" (ESV). We know from the Genesis 1 account of creation that when God was making each day, that after God made each day, He would look at what He had accomplished, and said it was "good." On the seventh day, when He was finished, He declared in reference to His entire creation that it was "very good."

From these Scriptures, you can conclude that God has designed and arranged every day. Whether God is creating or scheduling our days, the intended outcome is for your "good." Therefore, within each day is a pocket of His goodness that He wants you to discover. If you can discover it, it leads to some genuine rejoicing and gladness. In order to discover this good, however, you have to look beyond the temporal and see the eternal. It's my belief that we miss some of God's best because it comes disguised as something negative or difficult. If you can learn to recognize the disguise, then you can get in on the good that everyday carries for you.

Isaiah 45:3 is one of the many scriptures that communicate this truth: "I will give you the treasures hidden in darkness." The *New King James Version* says it this way: "I will give you the treasures of darkness." The word *darkness* simply describes the container, the word *treasure* describes the content. The implication is that though the container is dark, the content it carries is of great value. In fact, the *New English Bible* translates that phrase this way, "I will give treasures from dark vaults."

The key is not to be fooled by the darkness, but rather to realize that it is just a container God uses to bring us His treasures. If we ask Him, He will help us sift through the darkness until we find these treasures. Therefore, for a Christian, there is no such thing as a bad day. Please hear me, I am not saying that there aren't days that look bad or there aren't days that feel bad or there aren't days where bad things happen. What I am saying is that for a Christian, "bad days are good days in disguise." Psalm 34:8-10 gives us some further insight and instruction in regards to this principle:

> (8) O taste and see that the Lord is good; how blessed is the man who takes refuge in Him! (9) O fear the Lord, you His saints; for to those who fear Him, there is no want. (10) The young lions do lack and suffer hunger; but they who seek the Lord shall not be in want of any good thing."

In order to understand this passage, let's examine it more closely.

Verse eight addresses an individual because it says, "How blessed is the *man*." We also know that this man is in some kind of trouble because he is someone who is in need of *refuge*. It may be trouble because of a lost, a backslidden, or an immature state of life. To this person in need of refuge, an invitation is extended and that is to come "taste of the Lord and you will find that He is good." The psalmist is using the analogy of taste to communicate to us how God initially deals with us.

Our taste buds have been designed by God to help us easily and immediately determine whether something is good to eat or not. If you take a swig of sour milk, you don't need to swish it around in your mouth in order to determine whether or not the milk is sour. As soon as the milk goes into your mouth, your taste buds communicate to get it out. If there is a sink nearby, fine, but even if there isn't, the milk is still coming out. You would much rather go through the trouble of cleaning the mess up than keep sour milk in your mouth any longer than necessary. Your taste buds easily and immediately determined that the milk was bad.

In the same way, God initially deals with us in a like manner even though we might be in a lost, a backslidden or immature state of existence. We can both easily and immediately know that the God in whom we took refuge is a *good* God. God initially meets us where we are at and tailors His dealings with us so that no matter what state we are in, we can perceive His goodness.

However, in verse nine, a transition takes place. God is no longer talking to an individual, but to a community of believers. We know this because it says, "O fear the Lord you His *saints*." These are the ones who "tasted the Lord," found Him to be good, and decided to follow Him in order to continue to experience His goodness. To these saints, God doesn't extend the invitation to taste in order to experience His goodness, but they are given the command "to seek" in order to find His continual goodness. Verses nine and ten tell us that the goodness of God is still available, but it is no longer a matter of tasting, it is now a matter of seeking.

When you first meet the Lord, His goodness toward you can be overwhelming. He saves, fills, delivers, and blesses you. The good you experience is immediate and easily detected. However, as you begin to grow in the Lord, something happens to the good that you first experienced. It seems like either God slows down the rate at which He dispenses His good to you or the good He is dispensing isn't as readily apparent. When you first encounter the Lord, all you have to do is "taste" and you will reap His goodness, but as you grow, you are required to "seek" the Lord for the good He has for you. Christian maturity is allowing God to wean us from the tasting stage so we can move into the seeking stage.

Romans 8:28 states, "We know that God causes all things to work together for good to those who love God." To understand this verse, we need to realize that the Lord is not bound by our definition of what is good. God has one of His own. We think of good in terms of something pleasant and immediate. God thinks of good in terms of something enduring and ultimate, which may involve some short-term suffering. I have found that God doesn't mind me going through a little pain now in order to keep me from a whole lot of pain later. In other words, the Lord is more interested in the production of character than in the provision of comfort. Comfort is nice, but character is better. Often God will sacrifice your comfort in order to produce His character in you. Remember, this verse doesn't say that all things are good; it says that God is at work for good in all things.

Recently, I baked a cake from scratch and was amazed at the number of ingredients that go into a cake that by themselves don't taste very good. Vanilla extract, egg whites, baking powder, baking soda, and shortening all taste bad, but when I worked them together with some other ingredients, they don't taste so bad. Then I applied some heat, eventually the buzzer went off, and it came out tasting good.

Before I go any further, I need to point out that the heat of oven is a very important part of the process, because it is the heat that causes the metamorphosis. That being said, I want you to know that the Lord has better culinary skills than I do. He can take things that are in and of themselves bad and so work and mix them together with some other ingredients, like His grace, mercy, power, and providence, and the end result is something good.

However, you can't get to the provision of His good-ness without going through the process of His goodness, which includes the "oven" heat of life's challenges and trib-ulations. I've been at this so long now that I actually get ex-cited when I realize I am in the "oven stage" of the process, because I realize this is the last stage, and any time soon the buzzer is going to go off and that which was bad will have been transformed into that which is good.

Jesus' words in Matthew 7:7-11 give us further insight into how bad days are actually good days in disguise. Let's look at this passage verse by verse, in order to gain a deep-er, more thorough understanding of what is stated. Before I talk about "asking and receiving," let me issue a disclaimer here. I am taking for granted that I am communicating with someone who understands when I am talking about asking God for things, I am talking about those things that God has revealed in Scripture—those things He wants us to have. Those things would include deliverance, peace, joy, and pro-vision of our daily human needs. I don't believe you can ask God to help you win the lottery and He will hear and grant your request. That being said, let's examine this passage:

> (7) Ask and it will be given to you; seek, and you will find; knock, and it will be opened to you. (8) For everyone who asks receives, and the one who seeks finds, and to the one who knocks it will be opened. (9) Or what person is there among you who, when his son asks for a loaf of bread, will give him a stone? (10) Or if he asks for a fish, he will not give him a snake, will he? (11) So if you, *despite* being evil, know how to give good gifts to your children, how much more will your Father who is in heaven give good things to those who ask Him!

Verse seven states, "Ask, and it shall be given to you; seek, and you shall find; knock, and it shall be opened to you." I want you to notice how emphatic and specific this statement is. It says if you ask God for something, you will receive it; if you seek God for something, you will find it;

and if you knock on a door of opportunity, it will open to you. It doesn't say you might, could, or should; it says you will. The reason I emphasize this is because some Christians believe that our receiving from God hinges on what we are or are not doing. They believe it is their actions that either qualify or disqualify them for God's provision.

As Jesus was speaking, I believe He began to perceive that the people were beginning to disqualify themselves for this promise. They may have been thinking, *As soon as my marriage gets better, then I'll be able to ask and receive* or *As soon as I get out of debt, then I'll be able to seek and find,* or *As soon as I deal with my anger, then I'll be able to knock and the door will be opened.* I believe this is because of what Jesus said in verse eight. It is one of the few times in the Bible where Jesus repeats Himself. He says exactly what He said in verse seven except for the first two words "for everyone." Verse eight is the Lord's attempt by His grace to include everyone who had tried to disqualify themselves due to their performance.

One of the problems some Christians have is they don't understand the basis on which God gives what He gives. It's my premise that God's giving depends on who He is, not on who we are. All His giving is spurred by His goodness and not ours. James 1:5 gives us some insight into this attribute of God: "If any of you lacks wisdom, he should ask God, who gives generously to all without finding fault, and it will be given to him." This verse not only deals with what has been asked for, which is "wisdom," but also how God responds to all our asking, which is "generously and without finding fault." I don't care how pious you may be, or how long you have been a Christian, if the Lord was ever to look for a reason or a fault to not bless you, He wouldn't have to look very long or far. If not having faults was a condition for His giving, then none of us would ever receive anything.

When God seeks to give us something, He has to do two things; He has to overlook our past *and* overlook our future. God neither gives based on whether we deserve it nor on what we are going to do with it. Again, if He did, then none of us would ever receive anything. I have never deserved the things God has given me and, to be quite honest

with you, I have not always done right by the things He has
given me. There have been faults prior to His giving, faults
in the midst of giving, and faults after His giving. God knew
all this, and He still gave them to me anyway. Knowing this
should cause you to re-include yourself into the group of
"for everyone."

Because there is a lot of misunderstanding in this area
of "asking and receiving," I must put another disclaimer here,
so you won't misunderstand me. You may think, *Jim, if all of
that is true, then why should I behave or develop character if God is
going to bless me regardless of who I am or what I do?* Please hear
me. I'm not saying that behavior and character don't matter, for they do. I am saying they have very little to do with
getting the blessing, but everything to do with keeping the
blessing. Getting blessed is easy because it mostly depends on
God but staying blessed is difficult because it mostly depends
on us. Let me illustrate this by telling you a personal story.

As I mentioned in the first chapter, I spent eight years
of my life in prison. There were times when I attended a
chapel service when I was burdened with the weight of my
time, the separation from my loved ones, and my continual
failure to live up to my Christian convictions. In the midst
of the service, as I would seek God, He would meet me, lift
my burdens, comfort my soul, and encourage me to continue on. As a result, I would come out of the service filled
with His joy and peace. By that night, however, or maybe I
could make it to the next day, I would be back in the same
place I was before I went to the service. When this happened,
I would cry out to God, "What happened to my joy and
peace?"

In the midst of one of these cries, I heard God speak
by the still small voice these words, "You leak." I repeated,
"I leak?" And He said, "Yes. When you got angry with your
cellmate, some of your joy leaked out. When you got an
attitude at one of the guards, some of your peace leaked
out. When you dwelt on your future here, some of your joy
leaked out." I began to realize that developing character is
what fills those leaks and helps me keep what God has given
me.

Verses nine through eleven tell us that if you ask God for something good, you will receive the good for which you asked: "Which of you, if his son asks for bread, will give him a stone? Or if he asks for a fish, will give him a snake? If you, then, though you are evil, know how to give good gifts to your children, how much more will your Father in heaven give good gifts to those who ask him!" Let me re-iterate. It doesn't say you *might*, *could*, or *should* but that you *will*. Now you may say that you have at times asked God for good things, but you didn't receive them. My response to that is, "Yes you did, but you didn't recognize them when they came." The good you asked for wasn't easily detected because it came to you disguised as something you thought was negative—or it was shrouded in darkness. Therefore, you didn't recognize the answer to your prayer. I have found that praying is dangerous because God answers prayer. The danger is found in the way He chooses to answer your prayers.

These verses go on to say that if you ask God for bread, He won't give you a stone. If you ask Him for a fish, He won't give you a snake. However, often the bread you ask for comes disguised as a stone. It looks like something that is hard and painful, instead of something that heals; it looks like something that will damage you, instead of something that will deliver you; it looks like something that will harm you, instead of something that will help you. As a result, you reject God's answer instead of acknowledging and embracing it. If you aren't able to detect the disguise, then you lose out on the bread for which you were seeking. Let me give a few other illustrations to reinforce this point by telling you three stories of things that happened to me in prison.

SAVED THROUGH THE FIRE

As I mentioned in chapter one, I was saved one night and turned myself in the next day. Two months later, as I stood before the judge, I was convinced God was going to do good for me. My definition of good meant I was either going to get probation or a minimum sentence. I'm sure you will agree with me when I tell you that when the judge said 30 years, it looked like a stone to me. In the next couple of days in the midst of my prayers trying to work through this, God challenged me to see through the disguise and find the good it contained. It wasn't a stone designed to harm me but bread to nourish me. Because of that challenge, I began to realize I didn't need to get out of jail as much as I needed to get out of me the things that got me into jail.

I liken what happened to me during my incarceration to what happened in the story of the three Hebrew children found in the book of Daniel. In Daniel 3:4-6, we read that King Nebuchadnezzar issued an edict concerning an image which he created:

> "This is what you are commanded to do, O peoples, nations and men of every language: As soon as you hear the sound of the horn, flute, zither, lyre, harp, pipes and all kinds of music, you must fall down and worship the image of gold that King Nebuchadnezzar has set up. Whoever does not fall down and worship will immediately be thrown into a blazing furnace."

Three of the Hebrews who were taken captive, Shadrach, Meshach and Abed-nego, refused to bow down, so they were taken into the king's presence, where he gave them another opportunity to obey his edict. They replied with this courageous and bold statement,

> "O Nebuchadnezzar, we do not need to give you an answer concerning this matter. If it be so, our God whom we serve is able to deliver us from the furnace of blazing fire; and He will deliver us out of your hand, O king. But even if He does not, let it be known to you, O king, that we are not going to serve your gods or worship the golden image that you have set up" (Daniel 3:16-18).

What I want you to see in this statement is that they were counting on God delivering them from the fiery furnace. They were hoping that as they stood their ground and did what was right, God would then send down a team of angels who would blow out the fire and subdue the king and his soldiers. However, that didn't happen. In fact, this bold and courageous statement made the already angry king even angrier. He then heated the fire seven times hotter, and then had them bound hand and foot and thrown into the fire. The soldiers who bound them and carried them to the fire were immediately burned to death, but something miraculous happened to Shadrach, Meshach and Abed-nego:

> Then Nebuchadnezzar the king was astounded and stood up in haste; he responded and said to his high officials, "Was it not three men we cast bound into the midst of the fire?" They answered and said to the king, "Certainly, O king." He answered and said, "Look! I see four men loosed and walking about in the midst of the fire without harm, and the appearance of the fourth is like a son of the gods!" (Daniel 3:24-25).

These Hebrew children were not delivered *from* the fire but *through* the fire. Because they did what was right, when they were thrown into the fire they met Jesus in the midst of it. He shielded them from the damage of the fire, which then allowed them to appreciate the benefits of the fire. Instead of the fire *frying* them, it *freed* them. The fire burned off all their bounds, and they were loosed, able to walk around in the fire. Notice they didn't walk out of the fire but remained in the midst of the fire. I find it remarkable that they made no attempt to get out of the fire but only came out when the king summoned them! When you meet Jesus in your fiery ordeal you aren't that anxious to come out of it, because you realize all the benefits from it.

I too had done what was right. I turned myself in and confessed my crime. I was hoping God would deliver me from my fiery ordeal and grant me probation or a minimum sentence. Like the three Hebrew children, however, I wasn't delivered from the fire. Instead, I was delivered through the fire. I met Jesus in the midst of my 30-year sentence, who shielded me from the damage of incarceration, which enabled me to find the benefits of incarceration. All the fire of my incarceration did was burn off what bound me. It burned off my drug addiction, my alcoholism, and my arrogance, just to name a few of the things that had me bound. What looked like a stone to me was actually bread. What looked like a bad day to me was actually a good day in disguise. My testimony is that my 30-year sentence was the best bread I ever ate, and now years later, I am still walking in the nourishment that my eight years in prison afforded me.

ONE MEAN PRISON GUARD

After I was sentenced, I went back to my cell in the county jail disillusioned and disappointed, but God assured me He was doing what was best for me. When I accepted that I was going to be in prison for a long time, my prayers changed. Instead of praying to keep me from prison, I now started praying that God would help me survive prison. I had always been a rebellious and disobedient guy. It was my nature when an authority figure told me to do something, I would always do the opposite. I knew that if I was going to make it through prison, I was going to need God to help me to walk the straight and narrow—to dot all my i's and cross all my t's. Therefore, I started praying that God would help me be obedient and submissive to authority.

I don't know how I thought God was going to answer that prayer (remember I told you that praying is dangerous because of the way He chooses to answer prayers). Maybe I thought the next time I had an urge to disobey, God would zap me with an electric shock, or He would change me so I would instantly want to obey. Well, neither one of those things happened. The next day, when the guards woke me up at 5:00 a.m. and made me get out of bed, I said the same rude and rebellious things I had said the day before. I kept praying, but nothing seemed to be happening. Eventually I was taken to the prison where I was to serve most of my time, one of the worst prisons in the state of Florida. Not only were the inmates mean, but so were the guards.

There was one particularly mean guard who took a special disliking to me. This guard was so mean that the inmates gave him the nickname "Heater" because every time he was around, things would heat up. He felt my Christianity was a sham and he took it upon himself to prove that truth not only to himself, but to me and the others as well. Therefore, he made my life miserable. Every day he would seek me out and examine everything about the way I dressed and carried myself, in hopes of finding something wrong so he could write me up—which would lengthen my time before I would be eligible for parole.

Twice a week he would come to my rack (bed) looking for contraband for the same reason. While looking for contraband, he would break or damage the few personal items I had. For a whole year, I lived under the tyranny of the Heater. Finally, I got down on my knees and prayed this prayer: "Father, this year has been the most difficult of my life; not only because I am in prison, but even more so because of the presence of the Heater in my life. Father, I don't think I can do another year with his continual harassment. He is getting old, if you could cause him to take early retirement, that would really help me." Immediately, I sensed God speak these surprising words to my heart: "Son, make up your mind. You asked for help to walk the straight and narrow; you asked for help to dot all your i's and cross all your t's. I bring you someone specifically designed to do that and now you want me to remove him?"

I realized in a flash that for the past year, I had lived obediently and submissively to authority. God knew I needed a presence in my life like the Heater to impose discipline until it became self-discipline. Once I realized that the Heater was the answer to my prayer, I quit dreading his presence and started delighting in it. Instead of him seeking me out every day, I sought him out. I did this because what had looked like a stone was actually bread. What I thought at first was a bad day, was actually a good day in disguise.

A VULGAR INMATE

After being in prison for a while, I discovered a few things about myself that were incompatible with my Christianity. The first thing was that I didn't like lost people. Even though I had been lost and God loved me, I found it difficult to love the lost who were around me. At first, I justified this lack of love by rationalizing that people in prison were really lost. How could I love people who were trying to rape me or take advantage of me in other ways? The second I discovered was that I was racist. I was put into a prison with a population of 800 men and two thirds of them were black and thus, the white inmates were a minority. That meant they got the short end of the stick in most things. To summarize, I didn't like lost people and I didn't like black people, so if you were lost and black, I *really* didn't like you.

I knew enough to know that Jesus not only loved the lost, He loved *all* people of every nation, tribe, and tongue. Therefore, I started praying what I thought was a safe prayer and that was for God to make me more loving towards lost and black people. Again, I didn't know how God was going to answer that prayer. I guess I thought that one night, He would send a team of angels down to my bunk and infuse me with His agape love. Then I would wake up the next day overwhelmed with love for all people. Unfortunately, that didn't happen.

Every day I continually woke up with the same lack of love and feelings of prejudice I had before I prayed. The answer to this prayer came in the form of a new bunk partner. Up to that point, I had a Christian with whom I got along well, but in his place, I got the most belligerent, obnoxious, foul-mannered, black heathen you would ever want to meet. I knew of this man by his reputation and what I knew scared me. When he first met me and realized I was his bunk partner, he got a smile on his face, called me "momma," and started flirting with me. When he did that, it just reaffirmed in me why I didn't love lost people or black people. To make matters worse, he would invite all of his friends over to his bunk to play cards, and while they were playing, he would talk about what he would like to do to me sexually if he ever had the chance. He would talk like that while I was on the bottom bunk trying to read my Bible and pray.

After a week of this, I prayed that God would remove this vulgar man from my life. Again, I heard the Lord say, "Make up your mind. You asked to be made more loving, so I bring you someone who is specifically designed to cultivate in your heart love for lost and black people. Now you want Me to remove him?" This did not look like the bread for which I had asked, but like a stone that should be avoided—or tossed away!

I had much to learn. I didn't know love is a fruit and not a gift. Therefore it has to cultivated, not granted. If a person wants to be more loving, God will bring some unlovable people into their life in order to grow their love. When I understood my cellmate was bread disguised as a stone, I accepted him and in turn reaped the good for which I had asked. This man, whose name was Jesse, eventually became one of my best friends. It was through our friendship I learned that people who deserve love the least need it the most. I also learned that the people who seem hardest on the outside can be the most pliable on the inside. Finally, I learned that only hurting people hurt others, for it is out of their own pain that they inflict pain.

People like Jesse need someone in their life who will endure the pain being inflicted while ministering to the pain of the one doing the inflicting. Once their pain has been ministered to, not only will they stop hurting, they will also stop inflicting hurt on others. Jesse at first looked like one of the worst days of my life, but once I realized it was a disguise, I reaped from him some of the best days of my life.

I pray the next time you have what you believe to be a bad day that you will remember it is just a disguise. It is really bread that only looks like a stone. It's really a treasure hidden in some form of darkness. Don't run from it but run to it. Don't dread it, but delight in it. Don't reject it, but embrace it, knowing that "God causes all things to work together for your good."

THREE

A FLOWING RIVER IS SELF-PURIFYING

*God's way of using mission
to others as a way to produce
maintenance for you*

One of the passions I carry, and one of the callings I have been given, is to see the church move from a maintenance mode into a mission mode. A maintenance mode is the state of wanting to live for God primarily for the benefits of personal blessing. It's where the blessings of God have become the primary motivation for all service to God. In a maintenance mode, you read your Bible, pray, go to church, and tithe so God will continue to bless your life, marriage, family, and finances. A mission model is the state of living for God primarily for the purpose of being the blessing of God to others. It's when your motivation for wanting to be blessed is primarily so you can be equipped to be a blessing to others. It's also when you want to receive so you have something to give to others. Finally, it's when you freely give up your own rights for the good of others, because you discovered it is far better to serve your neighbor than to have your neighbor serve you. Sooner or later, all Christians should come to the realization that we minister to the lives of others at the cost of our own.

An example in the Scriptures of someone who went from a *maintenance* to *mission mode* is found in the story of the prodigal son in Luke 15:11-32. For our purposes, let's just look at a few verses that show how the younger son moved from a desire to be blessed to a desire to be a blessing. Luke 15:11-12 states, "A certain man had two sons; and the younger of them said to his father, 'Father, give me the share of the estate that falls to me.' And he divided his wealth between them." I want to read into the word *younger* the idea of immaturity for it was immaturity that caused him to see his father primarily as a source of blessing. The words *give me* indicate his desire for personal fulfillment and the promotion of self-interest.

Verse 13 reveals much about his selfish motives, for after receiving the blessing, he gathered his possessions and left the source of his blessing: "And not many days later, the younger son gathered everything together and went on a journey to a distant country, and there he squandered his estate in wild living." People who primarily serve God to get their needs met will abandon their God to some degree after their needs are met. Deuteronomy 6:10-12 addresses this tendency to forget the Lord after He has blessed us:

> "When the Lord your God has brought you into the land he promised your ancestors, Abraham, Isaac, and Jacob, and when he has given you great cities full of good things—cities you didn't build, wells you didn't dig, and vineyards and olive trees you didn't plant—and when you have eaten until you can hold no more, then beware lest you forget the Lord" (TLB).

Also in verse 13, we notice that once he left the presence of his father, he also left the protection of his father. Therefore, the inheritance which was given to bless his life became a burden that cursed his life.

Not only did he squander the blessing, but the blessing squandered him. Proverbs 20:21 tells us that "an inheritance gained hurriedly at the beginning, will not be blessed in the end." When we get a blessing and we mishandle it, it will mishandle us. I have discovered that getting blessed is easy mainly because it depends on God. Staying blessed is difficult mainly because it depends on us. Getting blessed primarily depends on God's generosity, staying blessed primarily depends on our character. This blessing that the prodigal thought would bring him to new heights in reality brought him to new depths.

As he is sitting in a pig's pen, where the pigs ate better than he did, the Bible says, "he comes to his senses" and remembered his father's house. In the midst of this memory, he got a great revelation. It was a revelation and it's one sufficient for any and all prodigals to get out of the pigpen where the pursuit of self-interest had gotten the best of him. The revelation was "in his father's house, the servants have more than enough." In the kingdom of God, servants always have more than enough, the reason being that a servant is someone who orients his whole life around that which will bless others. Servants understand the abundance of life is not for them, but for others. Servants are given enough for their own needs, then they are given some more which they know is for the needs of others. Therefore, a servant can be entrusted with the "more."

Once the prodigal got this revelation, he saw his father in a different light, realizing that the true inheritance his father had was not what he could give him, but rather what he could make him into. He realized that the riches of life had very little to do with what you have, and everything to do with who you are. Therefore, in verse 19, he came back to his father with a mature request, simply asking to be "made into a servant." He had moved from "give me" to "make me," and from "bless me" to "make me a blessing." Or another way of saying it is he went from a "maintenance mode" to a "mission mode."

Many Christians are sitting in churches warming pews, waiting for the mythical day when they are ready to do something for the Lord. The reason I call it a mythical day is because just like no one can get strong by watching someone exercise, you can't get ready in a pew. Your reasoning may be that you are not qualified to get it out until you get it right, that you need to live and be, before you go, do, and say. The problem with this thinking is you divorce yourself from the very dynamic which is designed to get you right. It's only as you get it out that you can get it right.

MIGHTY IN BATTLE

Hebrews 11:32-34 describes how God took a group of weak men and made them strong as they engaged the work of the Kingdom,

> And what more shall I say? For time will fail me if I tell of Gideon, Barak, Samson, Jephthah, of David and Samuel and the prophets, who by faith conquered kingdoms, performed acts of righteousness, obtained promises, shut the mouths of lions, quenched the power of fire, escaped the edge of the sword, from weakness were made strong, became mighty in battle.

The very last phrase of this passage is insightful for it tells us they "became mighty in battle." Some Christians want God to make them mighty and *then* give them a battle; God's way is to put you in a battle which will then cause you to become mighty. I have found that it's not *knowing* the will of God that matures you but rather *doing* the will of God.

There's no question that some people in every church need a lot of maintenance and to release them into mission would be to invite problems and controversy. However, the danger in not doing so is to separate them from the very dynamic that brings about real maintenance. Just like a flowing river is self-purifying, so also a mission-oriented Christian produces sanctification of self (I am not implying they sanctify themselves but God does that work as they go and obey). I have discovered that the best way to get the Holy Spirit to do something in you and for you is to allow Him to do something through you.

Not to release young and immature Christians into mission is to lose out on one of the church's greatest sources of productivity. Proverbs 14:4 states, "Where no oxen are the manger is clean, but much increase come by the strength of the oxen." In 1986 I started a church in the city of Orlando, Florida. Our first year was a very difficult year in that no matter what I did, our group of about 30 people never increased. In seeking the Lord on why we were not growing, God used Proverbs 14:4 to communicate to me that I was more concerned about a "clean manger" than I was "increase." This concern restrained me from allowing young and immature Christians from doing anything in the church for fear they would cause problems or create messes.

It is true that *"oxen"* will create messes, but they will also produce increase. New believers, if not interfered with, will have a natural instinct to evangelize. They speak more from their inability to remain silent than they do from their preparedness to speak. Statistics have shown the vast majority of new Christians have been won to the Lord by new Christians. Another verse or concept that hinders us from releasing the oxen is found in 1 Corinthians 14:40, which states "Let all things be done decently and in order."

Some Christians put the emphasis on the phrase "decently and in order" which causes them to be cautious—sometimes too much so. Therefore, they limit what can be done in the Church since most things are initially done improperly and in a disorganized way. Very few things come out of the gate already proper and orderly. Maturity is the process of moving from the improper to the proper, and the chaotic to the orderly. In the spirit of increase, we need to put the emphasis on the phrase "let all things be done." As we get things happening, the Holy Spirit will not only bring decency and order to what is happening, He will also use what is happening to bring increase. I immediately saw an example of this when I began to release some of the oxen in our church to both make messes and bring increase.

There was one young and immature Christian in our church who had a real zeal for the lost. He was athletic and thought he could use that as means to witness to the lost, so he joined a city softball league. He befriended the man playing shortstop on his team and his girlfriend. One night when they were out together, this young Christian lost his temper and got into a fist fight with this man and ended up breaking his jaw. Talk about a mess! I was shocked when I was told about it the next day.

Believing I had heard from God and in His ability to redeem all our messes, I encouraged this young man to apologize and to keep seeking to be their friend. This young man visited the man in the hospital, paid for his medical expenses, went by and made sure his girlfriend had all her needs met, and over the course of three months he had a chance to lead them both to the Lord. He then started a Bible study in their apartment and over the next two years was able to lead twelve other people to the Lord. Not only was there increase brought to our church, there was also increase brought to his soul.

Of course, I am not advocating this as an evangelistic strategy, but I am showing how the Holy Spirit can work in and through new believers. And I am suggesting that when we keep our eye on the prize, which is serving and touching the lives of others, then God can use simple and even immature ways to achieve His purpose of reaching the lost.

Are you in mission or maintenance mode in your faith walk with the Lord? Are you looking for what you can get or give as you serve Him and others? If you focus on mission, He will give you the maintenance you need from sources you least expect. It is not thinking less of yourself but thinking of yourself less. When that happens, you are functioning as Jesus did, not coming to be served but to serve and give His life as a ransom for many. Let's see in the next chapter how this mission mode showed up in one well-known story from the public ministry of Jesus as found in John's gospel.

FOUR

WHO HAS YOUR LUNCH?

*God's way of sustaining you
is when you bring sustenance
to others*

In this chapter and the next, I want to look at the story of Jesus and the Samaritan woman found in John 4:1-42 and draw your attention to two things in the story. The first, which I will discuss in this chapter, is how in verses 1-34 even Jesus was able to find the maintenance He needed for His life as He engaged in His life's mission. The second, which I will discuss in the next chapter, is how in verses 35-42 Jesus was able to see past the trash of this Samaritan woman's outward life and discover the treasure that was within her life.

It would be helpful if you read John 4:1-34 in its entirety in order to completely understand all I want to say to you. For this book's purposes, let's just highlight a few points. Verses 3 and 4 warrant a closer examination and simply state that "He [Jesus] left Judea and departed again into Galilee.

And He had to pass through Samaria." This is significant for a few reasons. The first reason has to do with where He was going, and the route He chose to get there.

Jesus was leaving Judea and going to Galilee, and normally a Jew would take the long way around through Perea in order to avoid going through Samaria, even though that was the most direct route. Samaria was a region no good Jew would pass through if he could help it. Samaria was comprised of people of mixed origin and malcontents who practiced an unorthodox and idolatrous brand of Judaism. The Samaritans represented to the Jews everything they considered vile and contemptible. The word "Samaritan" was a derogatory word they used when they wanted to insult someone. For example, in John 8:48 the Jewish leaders referred to Jesus in this manner: "Do we not say rightly that You are a Samaritan and have a demon?" Even though Jesus didn't hold to these views of the Samaritans, He still would have taken the Perea route in order not to offend the people who were His primary ministry focus.

The second reason has to do with why He chose the Samaria route to get to Galilee. Verse four states, "He *had to* pass through Samaria." The *Amplified Version* translates it this way: "It was *necessary* for Him to go through Samaria," and the *Young's Literal Translation* says, "And it was *behooving* Him to go through Samaria." The Greek word that is translated in the English as *had to, necessary, or behooving,* is *dei. Vines Expository of New Testament Words* gives two definitions for this word. The first is *necessity in reference to what is required to attain some end.* The second is *necessity established by the counsel and decree of God.* Therefore the *had to* in this verse didn't come from the convenience of geography but from the still small voice of the Holy Spirit from within. Jesus knew as He passed through Samaria that He was going to run into a pocket of God's will. It was the Spirit sending Him through Samaria in order to encounter a divine appointment.

I am going to spiritualize this passage, because even though what I am about to say wasn't the writer's original intent, I believe the implication is there that the Holy Spirit still prompts Christians to go through Samaria. Going through Samaria represents anything the Holy Spirit prompts us to do that we find difficult, unpleasant, or inconvenient. There have been many occasions when I was going one way but I sensed the Holy Spirit prompt me to go another way. To obey the Lord with this course change would usually cost me a price I didn't really want to pay. I would have to set my agenda aside in order to embrace God's.

Verses five through eight go on to tell us about this divine appointment which Jesus encountered as He passed through Samaria. In verse six, we are told that "Jesus was weary from the journey." From this, we learn that Jesus was hungry, thirsty, tired, and depleted. He was, if you will allow me to suggest, in need of maintenance. Verses seven and eight give us two solutions to Jesus' condition. One was from His disciples and the other was from His Father. The disciples' solution was to have Him rest and get a drink while they went into the city to get Him some lunch. The Father's solution to His Son's condition was to send some lunch of His own making. This lunch showed up disguised as a Samaritan woman who was in more need than He was.

REST DISGUISED AS WORK

Jesus needed rest and it came disguised as work. Jesus needed maintenance and it came disguised as a missions opportunity. One of the things we can glean from this passage is that mission opportunities seldom come at convenient times. I wish they all came right after church on Sunday, or right after my quiet time in the morning, or even after I listen to a worship song in my car. At those times, I feel like an attack lamb. I'm inspired, edified, and encouraged. At these times, I look for the "Samaritan woman, a.k.a. a mission opportunity." Most of the time, however, no mission opportunities surface then.

Instead on Thursday, after some very trying days, which included arguments with my wife, disagreements with my children, struggles with my finances, and indulgences of my flesh, I hear the Holy Spirit say to me, "I want you to go through Samaria. There is a mission opportunity I want you to engage in." At this point I am thinking, "Where were You on Sunday after church or even Monday after my quiet time; I was ready for it then?" I have learned that when I am not up to the occasion, the Holy Spirit is. The Spirit purposely waits until I am emptied of what I can do so He can fill me with what He can do. I have found the Spirit has an easier time working through my weakness than through my strength. God's power always shows up best in weak people.

In verses 31 through 33, we find the disciples trying to get Jesus to eat the lunch they had brought. However, He explains to them that He had eaten some food they didn't know anything about. The reason He said this was because they wouldn't have recognized what He did as food or seen it as something nourishing. They would have seen it as something draining. Jesus explained that He has already eaten the lunch His Father sent. They knew something had to have happened because they had left a weary Jesus, but they came back to a rejuvenated Jesus. They left a hungry Jesus, and they came back to a nourished Jesus. They left a depleted Jesus, and they came back to an overflowing Jesus.

In verse 34, we see that Jesus said His food (nourishment, sustenance, replenishing, maintenance) came from doing the will (mission) of His Father. Jesus indicated there is something sustaining about doing the will of God. This verse implies that your nourishment comes from nourishing others; your sustenance comes from sustaining others; your strength comes from strengthening others; your rest comes from working for others; and your prosperity comes from prospering others. In other words, your maintenance comes from His mission.

The question to ask yourself is, "Who has your lunch?" The Lord has placed your maintenance right in the middle of a mission opportunity, for it's in mission that you will find all the maintenance you need. If you sow the Lord into someone else, you will reap Him for yourself. You will never bring Jesus to someone or to a situation without Him showing up for you as well. The Holy Spirit will never work through you without doing something to you. Let me illustrate this for you by telling you two stories from my life.

FROG

The first story is from my time in prison. I had been there for about a year when the zeal of my initial experience with the Lord began to wane. Whereas at one time I had a peace about my time in prison, I was then becoming anxious about it. Whereas at one time I had a sustaining sense of His presence, then He seemed to be a million miles away. After His manifest presence was gone, the things of the world started to become attractive to me again. Temptations that were gone started resurfacing and I found myself anxious, joyless, and fearful. I was in need of maintenance. I was sitting on my bunk, crying out to the Lord for a fresh touch of His Spirit but for some reason the more I prayed, the worse I felt.

As I was praying, I noticed (in prison you pray with your eyes open) a particular inmate by the name of Frog who I did not like because he was both a drug dealer and someone who ridiculed my faith. When I saw him, he was coming back from mail call when he sat on his bunk and opened his letter. After reading it, he did something uncharacteristic for a person like him—he cried. I surmised that he had gotten a "Dear John letter" from his wife, indicating she was going to divorce him. I wish I could tell you that at the thought of this man going through this pain, I was filled with compassion and understanding. Unfortunately, I was not. In fact, I actually felt excited that God was finally judging him for all his sins, especially the ones he committed against me.

While praying for a touch from God as well as finding joy in this man's pain, I heard the Holy Spirit say to me, "I want you to go through Samaria." By that, I sensed God wanted me to go and comfort Frog in his pain, instead of celebrating his pain. My first response, was "I rebuke you Satan." I knew it had to be the devil because I was the one who needed comforted; I was the one who was praying; I was the one who was living for the Lord faithfully; I was the one who deserved a touch from God, not Frog.

As I continued to pray, the Holy Spirit kept prompting me to comfort Frog. Finally, I decided to obey the Lord, not because I wanted Frog to be comforted, but just to get the Holy Spirit off my back. I got up and went over to Frog's bunk where he was sobbing with his face in his hands. I put my arm around him, and with no compassion in my heart I said, "Frog, Jesus loves you and wants to help you." The moment I said that, the glory of God fell on both of us. Not only was God helping Frog, but He was also helping me as well. Not only did Frog receive comfort but a few days later he got converted and I received a sustaining touch from the Lord. It was then I began to understand that when I get involved in His mission, I receive all the maintenance I can handle. Frog had my lunch.

I NEED A NAP

The second story occurred when I was pastoring a church in Orlando, Florida. In 1986, six years after I got out of prison, I started a church in the living room of my home. We began with four people and within three years, we had about 80 people. Each year in January, each member of the church was encouraged to fast in some way for the 21 days. Some people fasted sweets, others fasted meats, some even fasted TV. Being the pastor, I felt I needed to set the example, so I fasted solid foods, only partaking of water and some juices. On the last week of the fast, we had prayer meetings at the church from Monday to Saturday. I oversaw the meetings Monday through Wednesday, and my associate oversaw them Thursday to Saturday. Thursdays were an extremely busy day for me when I taught Bible classes at two different county jails. When I got home that night, I was extremely weak and tired, but I was encouraged by the fact that there were only three days of the fast left, and I didn't have to oversee or attend the nightly prayer meetings. I was looking forward to a nice restful evening at home.

About 4:30 p.m., my associate called to inform me he had a family crisis and wouldn't be able to oversee the meeting that night. That meant I would have to lead it. I determined if I was going to do this, I needed a nap. I was just about to lay down, when the phone rang again. It was a couple from the church indicating that their baby was sick and they were taking her to the hospital. They asked if I could meet them there. If it would have been any other couple, I would have immediately said yes but this couple was very needy and demanding. They were a couple who drained the church emotionally and financially. This baby was their first child and they were quite over-protective. On more than one occasion, I went to meet them at a doctor's office or the hospital, only to find once I got there, they had already left since there was nothing wrong with the baby.

In light of the fact that I was tired, weak, and the chances were good there was nothing wrong with the baby, I was about to tell them no when I heard the Holy Spirit say, "I want you to go through Samaria." By this time, I had learned to respond more quickly to these promptings, so I got in my car, fought through Orlando traffic, and got to the hospital, only to find the couple had left. As I expected, there was nothing really wrong with the baby, but I knew God had sent me. It turns out they weren't my Samaritan woman—someone else was.

I found the nurse who had attended to their situation to inquire about the baby's condition. As we were talking, she asked me if I was the pastor who was supposed to come and pray. When I said yes, the nurse began to cry and told me of a situation in which she needed prayer. In my spirit I said, "Aha, the Samaritan woman!" I was able to minister comfort and hope to her soul. As I did, God ministered strength and power to me. His Spirit so quickened my body that when I got to the prayer meeting that night, I was fully alive in God. I got more rest from ministering to that nurse than I would have gotten from a two-hour nap. Again, when I got involved in His mission, I got all the maintenance I could handle. That nurse had my lunch.

The Lord wants to move you from a maintenance mode into a mission mode because in mission you will find all the maintenance you will ever need. Therefore, you need to be sensitive to the voice of the Spirit when He speaks in that still small voice and says, "I want you to pass through Samaria." As you pass through Samaria, I promise you will run into a mission opportunity. When you are obedient, two things will happen: Your mission will be accomplished and your maintenance will be received.

FIVE

GOD DOESN'T SEE THE TRASH IN OUR LIVES BUT THE TREASURE IN OUR SOULS

*God's way of bringing
the message to the worthless
and then using the worthless to
bring the message*

In the last chapter, we started to look at the story of Jesus' encounter with the Samaritan woman in John 4:1:42. From this story, I want to share two ways of God designed to produce two very important "acts of God," for your life. The first, which I discussed in the last chapter, was how Jesus found the maintenance He needed for His life as He engaged in His life's mission as described in John 4:1-34. The second, which I discuss in this chapter, is how He was able to see past the trash of the Samaritan woman's outward life to discover the treasure within her soul, which is found in John 4:35-42.

John 4:35 states, "Do you not say, 'There are yet four months, and then comes the harvest?' Behold, I say to you, lift up your eyes, and look on the fields, that they are white for harvest." The first phrase I want to look at is "lift up your eyes." Most commentators believe Jesus said this to draw His disciples' attention to the fact that a multitude of Samaritans were coming out from the nearby city led by the woman who had already received the light of the gospel.

The second phrase is "look on the fields." The Greek word for *look on* is *theaomai,* which means *to view attentively and to learn by looking.* It means you actually see and perceive what you are looking at. In this context, it means you move beyond a casual glance at the Samaritans' lives to a penetrating look into their souls. It means to see more than the obvious, with the idea of being able to see the sag that might be in their shoulders, the pain in their eyes, or even the desperation in their actions. Ultimately, it means to see past the sin in their lives to see the need in their souls.

In verse 35, Jesus was admonishing His disciples to see the harvest of these Samaritans in a different light. He was calling their attention to the fact that a vast number of souls which had been ripening all around them were now ready for reaping. He saw those Samaritans as being ripe for the picking. What Jesus saw when He looked at people like these Samaritans drew Him to those people. What the Pharisees saw repulsed them. What most people of His day saw as closed hearts, Jesus saw as open hearts.

This admonishment came immediately after Jesus successfully harvested a soul who everyone else would have missed. Think about it: Of all the places to find a hungry heart, He found one in Samaria. Of all the Samaritans to be searching for God, He found a woman. Of all the women, He found a five-time divorcee. She was an outcast of outcasts, the most insignificant person in that region. Yet He was sent to her. In the last chapter, I pointed out in verse four that "Jesus *had* to pass through Samaria." Not only was it amazing that someone like her was open to the gospel, but it was equally amazing that Jesus was able to detect her open heart.

He was able to do this because He saw the harvest

differently. He was able to see people differently. He was able to see sinners differently. Others would have seen a promiscuous Samaritan woman; Jesus saw the first fruits of a great revival. Others would have only given her criticism; Jesus gave her a chance. Others saw her as she was; Jesus saw her as she was intended to be. Others saw her promiscuity; Jesus saw her promise. Others only saw her problems; Jesus saw her potential. Others would have seen only trash; Jesus saw a treasure. He took a life that was drifting and gave it direction. He took a life that no one could use and used it as no one else could.

Throughout the gospels, Jesus always brought the message to the worthless and then used the worthless to bring the message. After bringing about conversion in her life, He released her to go back and do the same for others. He knew the best medicine for her problems was to get her involved in the problems of others. He knew that her maintenance would be found in His mission. For a moment, please humor me and imagine an angelic committee meeting in heaven to discuss the best way to evangelize this particular city in Samaria.

One of the options they discussed was finding a key person in the city, someone influential enough that if salvation was brought to their soul, he or she could be a catalyst to bring salvation to others. As they were contemplating who this person might be, one of the angels could have said, "Well, there is this overly friendly woman in the city who already has a network set up to spread her promiscuity. If we can turn her to the Lord, we can use that very same network to spread the gospel." Before you get too religious on me, search out the gospels and you will find that usually when Jesus led someone to the faith, He didn't say, "Come and meet My friends" but instead, "Take Me to meet your friends." An example of this is the story when Jesus called Matthew the tax collector to be one of His disciples. In Matthew 9:9–13, we read,

> "Passing along, Jesus saw a man at his work collecting taxes. His name was Matthew. Jesus said, 'Come along with me.' Matthew stood up and followed him. Later when Jesus was eating supper at Matthew's

house with his close followers, a lot of disreputable characters came and joined them. When the Pharisees saw him keeping this kind of company, they had a fit, and lit into Jesus' followers. 'What kind of example is this from your Teacher, acting cozy with crooks and riff-raff?' Jesus, overhearing, shot back, 'Who needs a doctor: the healthy or the sick? Go figure out what this Scripture means: 'I'm after mercy, not religion.' I'm here to invite outsiders, not coddle insiders" (MSG).

We should not be surprised that Jesus would use a promiscuous woman to evangelize a city or call a hated tax collector to become His disciple, for the Lord has always taken the insignificant and the common and used them to produce the spectacular. In the Old Testament, He took an ordinary rod, had Moses extend it, and parted a sea; He told an army to lay down their swords, take up a song, and rout an army; and He took a common pebble, slung it, and slew a giant.

In the New Testament, He took a peasant boy's lunch, blessed it, and fed a multitude; He took some everyday mud, spit on it, and restored sight; and He took a rejected, promiscuous woman, spoke kindly to her, and brought revival to a whole city. We need to see that because our Lord is able to turn a stick into a scepter, a stone into a missile, a song into a weapon, a sack lunch into a feast, some saliva and dirt into a balm for the blind, and an immoral woman into an evangelist, then He can take us, with all our sin that hurts others, and turn us into a saint that can help others.

GOD SEES US DIFFERENTLY

Not only was Jesus able to see others differently, He was also able to see me differently. Early in my Christian walk, I was challenged to find a verse that best sums up both my testimony and my mission. The verse I found is in Jeremiah 15:19: "If you return, then I will restore you. Before Me you will stand; and if you extract the precious from the worthless, you will become My spokesman." This perfectly describes and summarizes my testimony because the Lord had to look past the vast worthlessness of my life, see the speck of something precious in my soul, and then go about the process of extracting it.

Humor me once again and let's go on an imaginary journey back into the past back to July 26, 1972. See me sitting in my living room contemplating suicide because I had just killed someone and at the same time picture the Lord sitting in heaven on His throne from where He made the proclamation, "Tonight is the night I save Jim Newsom's soul." With that proclamation, I can see the angels and the saints who have gone on before me responding in shock and saying, "You are going to do *what*? Lord, can't You see all the hurt this man has caused his family, his neighbors, and *everyone* who has ever come in contact with him? Lord, he just killed someone. Can't You see all the worthlessness of his life?" I can imagine, and I hope you can too, the Lord responding by saying, "Yes, I see all that, but I'm seeing something you are not seeing. Look very closely past his pride, past his selfishness, past his anger, and see that little speck of possibility and potential. That is how I originally created him to be. That part of him is very precious to Me, and if I can speak to and touch that, then what I see will come forth, while what you see will be done away with."

It's not only my testimony that God saw me differently, it's also now become my mission to help others grasp that God sees them differently as well. I have learned that the mission for our lives comes out of the testimony of our lives. Isaiah 51:1 states, "Listen to me, you who pursue righteousness, Who seek the LORD: Look to the rock from which you were hewn, and to the quarry from which you were dug." If you can see how you were dug by God, it will teach you how to dig for God. What delivers you will also direct you; what ministers to you will also move you; what feeds you will also focus you; what saves you will also send you; and what brings change to you will also bring change to others. Because I was dug from the quarry of drug addiction, repeated incarcerations, and a life of laziness and failure, I am now able to dig (deliver) the addicted, the incarcerated, and the unproductive.

Isaiah 45:3 tells how you too can "lift up your eyes" and view the harvest differently. It states, "I will give you the treasures hidden in dark vaults" (NEB). The Hebrew word for treasures is *O-tsaw,* which means *a depository, armory, granary, or storehouse.* The Hebrew word for dark is *kho-shek,* which means *ignorance, sorrow, misery, wickedness, destruction, and death.* When we combine the two definitions, we can see the Lord was saying there are a lot of people who are a depository of His glory. However, it's easy to miss this truth because these treasures are often hidden in vaults of ignorance, misery, wickedness, and other destructive habits and lifestyles that lead to death. This verse admonishes you not to let the darkness of the vaults fool you into thinking there can be nothing of value inside. These depositories can hold grain, weapons, and riches. Throughout history, some of the richest grain (Bible teachers) and most powerful weapons (missionaries) came out of the darkest of vaults (lives).

Jesus didn't see the darkness of the Samaritan woman's vault; He saw the treasure of her soul. The darkness without was the indicator for Him that there was a treasure within. The entrance to the vault was no problem for the Lord because He knew the combination to the door. Throughout the Gospels, Jesus went around opening locked and dark vault doors and releasing the treasures they contained. You can see this not only with the Samaritan woman, but also with Zacchaeus, Matthew the tax collector, the demonized man, Mary Magdalene, and many others. To view the harvest differently, you have to look past the darkness of peoples' lives to see the treasures of their souls. You must see that the darkness of the vault as an indicator of a treasure within and then ask the Lord for the combination or the key to the door. As you apply the combination, you will see the treasure released, and their lives transformed.

Another passage that will help you see others differently is found in 1 Samuel 16:6-7. Before we look at these verses, let me give you the context that led up to this passage. The Lord had decided to replace Saul as king over Israel. Therefore, He told Samuel to go to Bethlehem to the household of Jesse and anoint one of his sons as the new king. At this point, Samuel doesn't know which son to anoint. Jesse, who had eight sons, only gathered seven of them. I think he only gathered his sons who looked the part of a king. David, the absent son, was the youngest and the least. What's more, he was a musician and a poet, which might have been an embarrassment for his father since they were not exactly the qualities one would look for in a king of that day. In any event, because of his outward appearance and stature, he was not invited.

In verse six we read that when the sons were brought before Samuel, Eliab, the oldest, immediately caught Samuel's attention causing him to think, "Surely the Lord's anointed is before me." Eliab must have had outwardly all the things a king should have, but the Lord spoke to Samuel and in verse seven and said, "Do not look at his appearance or at the height of his stature, because I have rejected him; for God sees not as man sees, for man looks at the outward appearance, but the Lord looks at the heart." The phrase I want you to notice is "for God see not as man sees." Once again, we learn that God doesn't see how people are as much as He sees how they could be. Paul admonished us in 2 Corinthians 5:16-17 to have this attribute of God:

> Because of this decision we don't evaluate people by what they have or how they look. We looked at the Messiah that way once and got it all wrong, as you know. We certainly don't look at Him that way anymore. Now we look inside, and what we see is that anyone united with the Messiah gets a fresh start, is created new. The old life is gone; a new life burgeons! Look at it! (MSG).

Just as we should not judge people by the clothes they wear, a book by its cover, or the contents of a gift by the way it is packaged, neither are we to judge the value of someone's soul by the sin we see in their life.

WOLFMAN

This point really came home to me when I was released from prison. Upon my release, I went to Gainesville, Florida to attend a two-year Bible school called Crossroads

School of Ministry. I chose this school because it offered classes in the evening and on Saturdays since I had to have a full-time job while on parole and could only attend classes during my off time. I also chose this school because it placed great emphasis on evangelism. Every Saturday, all the students and I were required to go on to the campus of the University of Florida and share our faith with the students we encountered. We didn't have to be on campus very long before we would run into one of the biggest drug dealers on campus. He was easy to spot because he was huge as well as long hair and a long, scraggly beard. The only name that I knew him by was his nickname, which was "Wolfman" who we learned was both belligerent and obnoxious.

Because of his persona and personality, I, along with most of the other students, kept our distance from Wolfman. From our viewpoint, he didn't seem like a very likely candidate for the Gospel. There was, however, a student at our school who was blind. When he was with us, he had someone lead him to a spot on the campus where there were plenty of bushes. He would then proceed to fall into the bushes on purpose. After he did this, he would then cry out, "Could somebody please help me! I'm blind. I've fallen into these bushes and can't get out." He would then share the gospel with whoever came to help him out, also inviting them to church.

Well, on one particular day the only person who heard his cries for help was Wolfman. The blind brother couldn't see that Wolfman wasn't a good candidate for the gospel, so he shared his faith with him, and invited him to church. You should have seen the expression on my face and the faces of some of the other students when the blind brother came into the church the next morning being led and helped by Wolfman. I wish I could tell you I was excited that Wolfman was in church, but I wasn't. I was still reacting to what I saw on the outside, which caused me to go to the head usher and have him and the other ushers watch Wolfman during the service. I further instructed them at the first sign of trouble to get him out of there.

However, Wolfman didn't cause trouble. He sat

intently during the whole service, and when the altar call was given, He ran forward and gave his life to Jesus Christ. Soon after that, he enrolled in the School of Ministry and graduated two years later. Within a year of his graduation, he took a team of twelve couples out to California and planted a church. That church today has more than 1,500 members. Wolfman, whose real name is George, is the senior pastor. I am ashamed to admit that a blind brother saw better than I did. All I saw was the outward appearance, but God enabled this blind brother to see this man's heart. I only saw Wolfman, God saw a senior pastor.

Not too long ago, I heard a story that illustrates this point even more clearly. A traveling teacher tells of being in a certain city where he was ministering at a particular church. After the Sunday night service, the leadership of the church took this minister into the city to get something to eat. As they were walking back from the restaurant to the parking garage, they passed a storefront doorway where a drunk wino had passed out. It was obvious by the way he was dressed and the stench of his clothes that he was a homeless person as well. This was a very awkward scene for these men. It was especially difficult for the traveling minister, because his father had been an alcoholic and there were plenty of times as a youth that he had found his father somewhere drunk and unconscious. Therefore, instead of feeling compassion for this man, he began to inwardly judge him.

In the midst of his judgmental thoughts, God spoke to him through His still small voice and said, "Don't you dare talk about one of My jewels like that." As this minister looked at this unkept, stench-ridden, homeless wino, he responded sarcastically, "*This* is one of Your jewels?" Whereby God answered back, "Yes, all he needs is a little polishing and guess who I am going to use to polish him up?"

After hearing this, the minister informed his companions what God had said to him and asked them if they could help him get this man back to his hotel room. The man who was driving said, "I don't want him in my car. He stinks" whereby this minister called a cab. The next morning as this minister was beginning to make plans to bring this wino back home with him, there was knock on his hotel room, and it was the men who were with him the night before. They said if God said that this man was one of His jewels, then they ought to be the ones that do the polishing, because he lived in their city. Today, as a result of God helping these men see this man not as he was but as he could be, this wino is now saved, restored to his family, and a deacon in the church.

What happed for George and this wino reminds of a cute little story I read not too long ago. It's about a six-year-old boy who had to walk through the park every day on his way home from school. As he did, he would pass an artist who was sculpting something from a big piece of granite. Every day the boy would stop for a few minutes and watch the artist at work. Several weeks went by, and one day as the little boy was passing through the park, the artist had finished his sculpture, and instead of a big piece of granite, there was a beautiful lion with magnificent detail. The little boy went up and asked the artist, "Sir, how did you know that there was a lion inside of that rock?" Though this story is cute, it is also true. The artist didn't see a big piece of granite. Instead, he saw a lion and all he did was sculpt what he saw.

When God looked at Wolfman, He didn't see a drug dealer, He saw a church builder. When God looked at the wino, He didn't see a drunk, He saw a deacon. And on July 26, 1972, when God looked at me, He didn't see a murderer, He saw a minister, and then He sent the Holy Spirit to sculpt what He saw—and He's been sculpting ever since.

SIX

GOD WILL FIX A FIX TO FIX YOU

God's way is to take the worst of times and use them to produce the best of times

"It was the worst of times and it was the best of times" is a quote from the book *The Tale of Two Cities* that, in my opinion, best sums up my Christian experience. The eight years of my life I spent in a Florida prison were filled with some of the worst times of my life because I was in prison, but they were also filled with some of the best times because I was in Christ. Over the years, I have discovered the worst and best of times are eternally linked. God uses the worst of times to break, mold, and shape you in order to bring you into the best of times.

Isaiah 45:3 states, "And I will give you treasures hidden in the darkness," meaning that the Lord will use the dark times of your life to bring you some of His greatest treasure. Jeremiah 15:19 further states, "Before Me you will stand; and if you extract the precious from the worthless, you will become My spokesman." Once again, you see in the midst of something that is seemingly worthless how God can and will help you find something precious. Jesus said in John 16:33, "Here on earth you will have many trials and sorrows; but cheer up, for I have overcome the world." Trials and sorrows will help you discover His overcoming power, which will then bring cheer into your life. The point is that in the midst of the worst of times, God will help you find the best of times.

The author of Hebrews wrote, "Let your character be free from the love of money, being content with what you have; for He Himself has said, I will never leave you, nor will I ever forsake you" (Hebrews 13:5). The phrase I want to focus on is *being content with what you have.* First, let me give you a few definitions for contentment: 1) rest or quietness of the mind in the present condition; and 2) satisfaction which holds the mind in peace, restraining complaint, opposition, or future desire. The *Amplified Version* states it this way: *be satisfied with your present circumstances.* It doesn't say be content if everything is going well or if everyone is feeling well or if everyone is doing well. The implication is that no matter what is presently happening in your life, you can find contentment.

In order to be content with what you have, you need to fully grasp what it is that you have. The rest of the verse goes on to say, "for He Himself will never leave you nor forsake you." The Greek word translated *content* is *arkeo*, which means *to be possessed of unfailing strength, to have enough, to be satisfied.* Contentment isn't based on what you have or don't have, but rather is based on who has you. You belong to Jesus who bought you at the price of His blood. Since Jesus has you, it means in turn that you have Jesus, and Jesus is and has everything you need. Jesus is enough. It's not Jesus plus good health, or Jesus plus a good job, or Jesus plus anything.

Paul understood this better than most. In 2 Corinthians 12:7-11, Paul described how God gave him a thorn in order to help him and went on to say that somebody from the enemy's camp gave him the thorn and was using it to buffet him. As a result, Paul asked the Lord to remove it on three different occasions. However, God responded to him with these words: "And He has said to me, 'My grace is sufficient [*arkeo*] for you, for power is perfected in weakness.'" The Greek word translated *sufficient* is the same Greek word translated *content*. Yes, Paul could be content with a messenger of Satan sticking him with a thorn because God's unfailing strength was with him, and for Paul that was enough. Paul knew that though the thorn would hurt (worst of times), it would also help (best of times).

You can be satisfied in your present circumstances because God's promise is that the presence of God will neither leave nor forsake you. The Greek word translated *leave* is *aniemi*, which means He won't relax His grip or loosen His hold on your life. It doesn't mean He will take you out of your present circumstances; it means He won't leave you while you are in the midst of them. Contentment comes when you know He's got a hold of you in your circumstances, and He will hold you while the circumstances mold you.

The Greek word translated *forsake* is *egkataleipo*, which means He won't leave you behind some place. The implication is that once the circumstances have done their work, God won't abandon you to them or leave you in them. Once they put something in, God will take you out. Once the circumstances have changed you, then God changes your circumstances. Paul wrote, "Godliness with contentment is great gain" (1 Timothy 6:6). The Berean translation says it this way: "Contentment with the things that produce godliness will yield great gain." If you understand this, then instead of running from the worst of times, you will remain in them because you know they will eventually yield the best of times. Then, instead of praying "deliver me from" your present circumstances, you will begin to pray "develop me through." Let's look at another passage Paul wrote:

> But I rejoiced in the Lord greatly, that now at the last your care of me hath flourished again; wherein ye were also careful, but ye lacked opportunity. Not that I speak in respect of want: for I have learned, in whatsoever state I am, therewith to be

content. I know both how to be abased, and I know how to abound: *everywhere and in all things I am instructed* both to be full and to be hungry, both to abound and to suffer need" (Philippians 4:10-12, KJV, emphasis added).

What makes this statement by Paul both profound and powerful is that when he wrote these words, he was in a Roman prison shackled between two Praetorian guards. He wasn't seeing the opposition, imprisonment, shackles, or loneliness; he was seeing only the opportunity that gave him time to write the churches and also to lead his guards to the Lord. His contentment came from not dwelling on what he didn't have but realizing what he did have. In verse 12, Paul gave us the secret to finding contentment in your present circumstances. He wrote, "everywhere and in all things I am instructed." The Greek word for *instructed* is *mueo*, which means *to initiate into the mysteries or knowledge of God.* The implication is that God has allowed your difficult situations in order to teach you something so until instruction takes place, provision or deliverance won't.

The psalmist wrote, "God is our refuge and strength, a very present help in trouble" (Psalms 46:1). After reading that you may raise the question, "Why didn't He help me out of the trouble?" That is not His order. He must first adjust you in the trouble and cause you to learn your lesson from it. His promise is "I will be with you in trouble." He must be with you in the trouble first, then He will take you out of it. God uses trouble to teach you precious lessons intended to educate and shape you. He doesn't regard them as difficulties, but as opportunities. Deliverance will not come until you have stopped being restless and fretful about the trouble, and become calm, quiet, and content. Then He will say, "It is enough."

There is a translation that words 1 Corinthians 10:13 this way: "God is faithful, He will not let you be tested beyond more than you can stand. But when you are tested, He will also make a way out" (Beck). I like this interpretation because the translator uses the word *test* instead of *temptation.*

If you see your difficulty as a temptation, Satan will use it to bring out the worst in you. If you see it as a test, God will use it to bring out the best in you. The word *temptation* causes most people to misinterpret this verse, which then causes them to focus on the last part of the verse, "the way out," instead of on the first part of the verse, "being able to stand."

Paul was saying that the faithfulness of God will not let you be tested or tempted beyond what you are able to handle. He implied that if something is on you, then you can handle it, no matter what your feelings, friends, or finances say. If for some reason you buckle under the test instead of standing in it, then God will provide "a way out." He does this because He will not let something He allowed in your life to help you instead to hurt you. Taking the way out will retard your spiritual growth, and somewhere along the journey, He will fix you up with the same test, hoping you will seek to be developed through it instead of being delivered from it.

A Bible teacher I knew once said, "God will fix a fix to fix you, but if you fix the fix before it fixes you, He has no other option but to fix another fix." Difficult experiences are designed to train and prepare you for a new movement of God's Spirit in your life, provided you enter the difficulty with a heart for God. Enter it with the wrong attitude, or if you simply search for an escape route, you will probably experience hardship and defeat.

EXAMPLES OF A GOD FIX

Two stories in the Gospels illustrate this principle. The first story is found in Mark 4:35-40 where Jesus told His disciples, "Let's go to the other side." As they got into the boat and launched out into the will of God, a furious storm (this is standing operating procedure) came upon them. Even though most of these disciples were seasoned fishermen who had been in storms before, this storm was so bad that they feared for their lives. This fear caused them to wake the Lord, who was asleep (even though it was stormy) and accuse Him of not caring about them. In response, He rebuked the storm and caused it to be still, then He rebuked the disciples for having no faith.

This story is not about God's ability to still storms, but about God's ability to keep His disciples in the midst of storms. The stilling of the storm was a result of the disciples having no faith. It was never Jesus' intention to still the storm but to set an example of how to get through the storm. He did that by resting in it and not running from it. Jesus was trying to teach them through the storm that they had no reason to fear because He was in the boat with them. When He is in the boat with you, no storm can hurt you. By taking the way out, they didn't learn the intended lesson.

The second story is found in Matthew 14:22-32. This story is another instance when the Lord told His disciples to "go to the other side" but as they did, another storm came upon them. Since they fixed the fix that was designed to fix them, the Lord fixed another fix. This time Peter decided that he was going to be instructed by the storm instead of seeking deliverance from it. As a result, he learned to walk on the very thing that had previously threatened him. Jesus didn't still this storm, but once Peter passed the test, the storm was stilled automatically. Once he was instructed by it, he was then delivered from it. The best way to still a storm in your life is to learn to walk on it or be instructed by it.

God wants you to learn contentment and teach you that He is enough. He will use difficulties and needs to instruct you. When I first began my prison sentence, all my efforts were spent on getting out of prison instead of allowing God to use prison to get something into (or out of) me. Then one day, the Lord spoke to my heart and said, "Son, I won't deliver you from prison but I will deliver you through prison." From then on, instead of looking for a life outside my circumstances, I was challenged to find His life in the midst of my circumstances. The life I found in the midst of the storm was better than anything I had experienced apart from it. This was so much so that four years later when I went to my parole hearing, I was praying I wouldn't get it. I had found a place of rest and instruction in the midst of the storm, and I didn't want out of it yet. Real contentment also comes from knowing you can't save yourself, as the following passage communicates:

"Who among you fears the Lord and obeys His
servant? If you are walking in darkness, without
a ray of light, trust in the Lord and rely on your
God. But watch out, you who live in your own
light and warm yourselves by your own fires. This
is the reward you will receive from Me: You will
soon lie down in great torment" (Isaiah 50:10-11).

This passage serves as a warning to those who walk
in darkness and do everything they can to help themselves
into the light. They are represented as individuals who start
a fire to warm themselves with the flames. This means that
when you are in darkness, the temptation is to find a way out
without trusting in the Lord and relying on Him. Instead of
letting Him help you out of the darkness, you try to help
yourself out. You try the using your reason and are tempted
to accept a way of deliverance which would not be of God at
all. You rely on a line of credit instead of on faith in God, or
you rely on the counsel of friends instead of the counsel of
God. These are fires of your own kindling. Do not try to get
out of a dark place, except in God's time and in God's way.

As I shared in past chapters, the time of trouble is
meant to teach you lessons that you sorely need. Job 36:15
states, "But those who suffer He delivers in their suffering;
He speaks to them in their affliction." Another translation
says it this way: "He delivers the afflicted by their affliction
and opens their ear by adversity." Remember, until instruction takes place, provision or deliverance won't take place.
Please know that premature deliverance frustrates God's
work of grace in your life. Be willing to abide in darkness
so long as you have the light of His presence. It is better to
walk in the dark with God than to walk alone in a light of
your own making.

Contentment is based on having a right understanding
of God's relationship with you. The first thing you should
know about God is that He knows all about you. He is the
one responsible for putting you together and making you
the person that is uniquely you. He knows all your thoughts
and is familiar with all your ways. He knows what will make

you happy and what will make you sad (see Psalm 139:1-18). The Lord knows how fragile you are (see Psalm 103:14). He is aware of your humanity and is more comfortable with it than you are. He knows your strengths and weaknesses and has promised not to put on you more than you can bear (see 1 Corinthians 10:13).

The second thing you should know about God is that He knows all your needs, not just your general needs such as food, drink, and clothing, as Matthew 6:7-8 and 31-32 states but also your personal specific needs such as your need for love; your need for understanding; your need for recognition; your need for adventure; your need for security; your need for acceptance; and your need for encouragement. The third thing you should know about God is that He has promised to meet all of those needs: "And my God shall supply all your needs according to His riches in glory in Christ Jesus" (Philippians 4:19). The key to understanding this verse is that "God will supply all of your needs." Who will supply your needs? It's not your spouse, your children, your job or career, and not your skills or talents. One of your problems might be that you have been looking to people and things to supply your needs instead of God. By looking to other sources, you will miss the ways God is wanting to meet your needs.

The fourth and last thing you should know about God is that He has the power to fulfill His promises: "Yet, with respect to the promise of God, Abraham did not waver in unbelief but grew strong in faith, giving glory to God, and being fully assured that what God had promised, He was able also to perform" (Romans 4:20-22). Also, Paul wrote in 2 Corinthians 9:8, "God is able to make all grace abound to you, so that in all things at all times, having all that you need, you will abound in every good work." This tells you that if you really believe God knows all about you, all of your needs and has promised and has the power to fulfill His promise and meet all those needs, then if the need hasn't been fulfilled yet, it's because you must not need it—yet. Again, the Bible says if you needed it, you would have it, whether that need is a friend, a physical healing, money, a marriage partner, a ministry opportunity, or any other of a myriad of needs we all have. Another way to state this is that what you have presently is what you need because if you didn't need it, you wouldn't have it.

Romans 8:28 is a familiar verse I am sure you know and quote regularly: "God is working everything together for your good." The challenge for you is that God is using His definition of what is good for you and not yours. A significant struggle when raising kids is to get them to believe they don't need certain things while they do need other things. God has the same struggle with you and me. God is your Father and you are His child, and you need to remember that there are some things you want right now but He knows you don't need them. There are other things you do have you don't want but you have them because He knows you need them. Your discontentment comes when you take the timing to meet your needs out of His hands into yours.

One of the less prevalent and desirable fruits of the Spirit is patience. God operates according to one timetable only and that is His! The following verses will testify to this.

> "There is an appointed time for everything. And there is a time for every event under heaven" (Ecclesiastes 3:1).

> "He has made everything appropriate in its time" (Ecclesiastes 3:11).

> "At the appointed time I will return to you" (Genesis 18:14).

> "He sent a man before them, Joseph, {who}was sold as a slave. They afflicted his feet with fetters, He himself was laid in irons; Until the time that his word came to pass, the word of the Lord tested him" (Psalm 105:17-19).

> "For while we were still helpless, at the right time Christ died for the ungodly" (Romans 5:6).

You can learn to be content with what you have when you realize you have Jesus. If you have Him, you can be content with anything. If you don't have Him, you can't be content with everything or anything. The secret of contentment is based in the knowledge that God will use the worst of times in your life to bring you into the best of times for your life.

SEVEN

WHAT TO DO WHEN YOUR PAST BEGINS TO CHASE YOU

God's way of using what is in your future to produce ministry for your past

There is a story told about a New York lawyer who went duck hunting in Tennessee. The first morning he was there, he shot a duck, but it fell in a farmer's field. As the lawyer was going into the field to retrieve his duck, the farmer who owned the field pulled up on his tractor and asked the lawyer where he was going. The lawyer told him he had shot a duck and was going into his field to get it. The farmer then replied that the field was his and anything that was in the field, including the duck, belonged to him. The lawyer informed the farmer that he was a lawyer, and that if he didn't get his duck, he would sue him for everything he owned.

The farmer replied that people around those parts didn't sue one another but rather settled matters by the "three-hit rule." The lawyer asked what that was and the farmer responded, "It's where I get to hit you three times and if you don't concede, then you get to hit me three times. If I don't concede, then we continue until one of us concedes." The lawyer looked at the farmer, who was up in age and frail looking, and figured since he was six feet four and weighed 240 pounds, the farmer was no match—so he agreed. The farmer came over and punched the lawyer in the stomach, which doubled him over, then he gave him an upper cut, and then finished up with a right cross. This left the lawyer bloody and reeling, but he was rejuvenated by the fact that it was his turn. As he approached the farmer, the farmer threw his hands up in the air and said, "That's alright. You can have the duck."

I wrote all that to say that too often we as Christians find ourselves fighting over ducks instead of fighting for eagles. A duck represents what interests me, but an eagle represents what interests God. We fight over temporal things instead of fighting for eternal things. We fight to preserve our lives instead of fighting to promote His life. Ephesians 6:11-12 states, "Put on all of God's armor so that you will be able to stand firm against all strategies and tricks of the devil. For we are not fighting against people made of flesh and blood." An effective strategy of the enemy is to attack the things that interest us so we will take our eyes off the things that interest God. If he is successful, he moves us from being a prophetic people to being a self-preserving people.

The other thing to keep in mind from the Ephesians 6 passage is that "our struggle is not with flesh and blood" and not with people. However, if you are like me, it seems that most of my struggles come housed in somebody who has flesh and blood, which means most of my fights seem to involve people. Just like the Father will use people to bless and help us, the enemy will use people to curse and hurt us. Too many times we are fighting the people the enemy is using, instead of fighting the enemy.

This became clear to me from another experience I had in prison. As most of you know, prison can be tough and inmates can be cruel. There was a particular week when I was in prison that was especially hard. I had just come from the infirmary where I had visited a brother who had been gang raped by a group of inmates. When I got to my bunk, I discovered that my locker had been broken into again and all of my personal stuff was stolen. On the tail end of that, I was told by another inmate that a group of inmates had just mugged my best friend who was in the infirmary. As you can imagine, I was quite angry, and as I sat on my bunk with my head bowed, I was feeling intense hatred for the unredeemed portion of the inmate population. In fact, in my mind I was visualizing going to a some of those inmates and beating them with a baseball bat.

As I sat and savored that scene in my mind, two things happened. The first was the realization that though I could beat these inmates with a bat, causing them to fall in defeat, the evil power and influence that caused them to do what they did would still be standing. On that day, I saw clearly the truth that "our struggle is not with flesh and blood but against the rulers, against the powers, against the world forces of this darkness, against the spiritual forces of wickedness in the heavenly places."

The second thing that happened to me that day was God allowing me to feel for a moment what He feels for the flesh and blood people who had just perpetrated all those crimes. He didn't feel hate but love; He wasn't wanting to fight them but forgive them; and He didn't consider them villains but victims. His love had the power to transform their wickedness into righteousness if they could just for an instant experience it. Just as the enemy had found someone to express his hate through, the Lord was looking for someone He could express His love through.

From that experience, I learned that people who deserve love the least need it the most and only hurting people hurt others. God is looking for someone who will look past the fact that someone is hurting them and realize that the one inflicting the pain is in pain. Then, while enduring their hurt, they minister to their pain. The result is that they stop inflicting pain since they are no longer in pain. In the New Testament, as in the Old, it seems men had to find somewhere to unload their anger, accusations, and complaints. If a good person is chosen as the whipping boy, it is only because a good person can take it. A good person, like a good God, can absorb all the hatred and abuse others may care to throw at them without it crushing them. Before evil can be conquered, it must be absorbed. Goodness has the power to absorb or swallow up evil. Goodness in the face of evil conquers it: "Do not be overcome by evil, but overcome evil with good" (Romans 12:21).

As described in Acts 14, Paul vividly demonstrated this principle for us. While in the city of Lystra, Paul preached the gospel through which half the city was revived and the other half rioted. They took Paul outside the city and stoned him to death. The brothers prayed over him and God raised him up. Then he did something that only someone with the heart of God could do, and that was he went back into the same city. He was more concerned about the people who stoned him than about the fact he got stoned. Paul realized that we minister to the lives of others at the cost of our own, that we can't sow our lives and preserve our lives at the same time. Paul decided not to fight over the things that interested him but to fight for the things that interested God.

Another strategy of the enemy involves the two ways through which he deals with the truth of God's Word. The first way is to try and blind you to certain truths in the Word of God. He will use your traditions, the way you were raised, your prejudices, or your emotional temperament to blind you to some legitimate and important aspects of God's Word. That's how he holds keeps you from the truth, or should I say the truth from you. Because of your deep hunger and desire for the Lord Jesus Christ and all He has, somewhere along the way you break free of his clutches and you are able to move into a new understanding of God's Word. You discover the power of the Holy Spirit, you discover who you are in Christ, and you discover your need for the Body of Christ. These new revelations both refresh and free you which causes you to move out of your complacency into His conviction, out of your mediocrity into His momentum. In fact, you are then moving in your Christian life in a way that you never moved in before.

Then the enemy deploys a different tactic, and that is instead of holding you back, he comes behind you and he pushes you into some extreme of the truth. The enemy knows that he can get you into error by either de-emphasizing certain aspects of God's Word or by over-emphasizing them. Either way, he negates God's Word. By de-emphasizing it, you disrupt it; and by over-emphasizing it, you distort it, ignoring this warning: "The man who fears God will avoid all extremes" (Ecclesiastes 7:18 NIV).

MEMORIES OF YOUR PAST

An example of what I am talking about is found in a particular aspect of counseling that a lot of Christians and churches practice today. Many years ago, the Holy Spirit began to add a counseling tool to the toolbox of the church. This particular tool has different names and is applied in different ways. Essentially, it is a therapeutic counseling technique where someone helps you to go through the memories of your past in order to bring healing and deliverance to your present.

Before I go any further, let me state that I believe this is a legitimate tool which the Holy Spirit initiates and empowers in order to help Christians. However, I also believe that the enemy has successively caused this tool to become distorted by the overuse of it. It was designed to be a tool for some situations, but has now become in the hands of some *the* tool for *most* situations. This tool has a place in dealing with sins and hurts, but it shouldn't have *the* place.

These problems happen because of the inability of Christians to handle either failure or success. When we fail, we want to quit. When we succeed, we want to duplicate and then market that success. The success was a result of God initiating and empowering some specific truth in order to heal and deliver us. We then make the mistake of thinking that because it worked for us in our situation, it will work for others in theirs. When we make that assumption, we fail to take into consideration timing, spiritual maturity, or temperament. From that moment on, we are doing the initiating, with the belief that God will automatically do the empowering. What started out as a "work of the Spirit" in us then becomes a "work of the flesh" through us. What began as a revelation became a technique.

In 1989, I went to Las Vegas, Nevada to visit with my brother after 18 years of estrangement. As I was flying out there, I was praying about how I could impact my brother's life. I sensed the Holy Spirit by a still small voice say to me, "Go where he takes you, don't ask any questions, and have a good time." After picking me up from the airport, my brother took me to a bar where he met up with his friends and began to drink. I hadn't been in a bar since I had met the Lord, but I had this "word" the Holy Spirit initiated, which proved to be empowered by Him as well.

As my brother and his friends drank alcohol, I drank Coke. When they told off-color jokes, I told clean ones, and my clean ones were funnier than their off-color ones. I enjoyed being with these men and they enjoyed being with me. I didn't join in their sin but I was involved in their lives. I didn't become like them but I was with them. As a result of this evening in a bar with men who drank, I was able to lead my brother and eventually a few of his friends to the Lord. However, I did not try to duplicate this success by taking license with this "word" and starting a "bar ministry." I haven't been in another bar since that time because I understand that the Holy Spirit will only empower what He initiates.

When Jesus walked the Earth, He never tried to duplicate the success of yesterday. Each miracle Jesus did was unique. At times He healed everyone, at other times He healed only one. At certain times He would heal in front of the crowd, at other times He would take the person off by himself. At times He spoke and people would be healed, at other times He would touch them but look at how He touched them. Once He put His fingers in someone's ears, another time He touched their tongue with spit, then on another occasion he made mud from His spit and rubbed it on their eyes, telling that person to go and wash in a certain pool. The reason for this variety is that Jesus never tried to initiate anything on His own. He said in John 5:30, "I can do nothing on My own initiative," and in John 5:19, "Truly,

truly, I say to you, the Son can do nothing of Himself, unless it is something He sees the Father doing."

If Jesus, the Son of God, couldn't do anything of His own initiative, do you think it's important for us to wait on God and then only do what He does? The reason God requires us to wait on Him to initiate what we do is two-fold. The first is that God loves variety as evidenced by His magnificent creation. The second is that He doesn't want us to depend on a technique, but on the Teacher; not on the revelations, but on the Revelator; not on the gifts, but on the Giver; and not on the things of God, but the God of the things. Just because He did something today for us one way doesn't automatically mean He will do it tomorrow for someone else in the same way. This keeps us dependent on Him, and not on a technique.

As stated earlier, a popular counseling tool utilized to-day is called "healing of the memories." This occurs when someone helps another go through the memories of their past in order to bring healing to their present. In my opin-ion, this tool is both overused and misused. Our healing and deliverance is never found behind us, but always in front of us. The past is valuable as a guidepost, but dangerous if used as a hitching post. As we move forward in our faith follow-ing God, He will lead us into circumstances and situations which have the power to deal with what is behind us. It's my position that the best way to deal with your past is by con-tinuing to move forward in your faith. There is something in front of you God wants to lead you into that will deal with what's behind you.

Jesus said in Luke 9:62, "No one who puts his hand to the plow and looks back is fit for service in the kingdom of God." Jesus in this verse sets the rule about looking back-ward into your past. He said, "Don't look back." However, like all rules there are exceptions, so at times under the ini-tiation and guidance of the Holy Spirit, with the help of a trained mature Christian, it may be necessary to look back into your past. When this happens, there is a danger because once the Lord brings healing to your life by looking back at your past, it's tempting to start treating the exception as though it was the rule. After a while, the exception of "looking back" becomes the rule, and the rule of "not looking back" becomes the exception. You can't afford to do that because in the same way a farmer can't plow a straight line if he looks backward, a Christian can't move forward in their faith if they are constantly looking back into his past. The more you look backward, the less you are able to see forward. Dwelling on your past will cause you to miss the direction God has for your future.

The above verse says "looking back" makes you unfit for God's Kingdom, or another way of saying it is searching through your past keeps you from serving His purpose. The Greek word that is translated into the English word *fit* is *eutletos*, which *Vine's Expository of New Testament Words* defines this way: *ready for use; well adapted; or well placed*. In other words, looking back into your past makes you useless for the future, clinging to the old, keeps you from being adapted to the new. You get out of place when you dwell on your yesterdays, but you become well placed when you look for His direction in your todays.

Paul, the most prominent figure in the New Testament other than Jesus, picked up on this principle in Philippians 3:13, which states, "No, dear brothers, I am still not all I should be, but I am bringing all my energies to bear on this one thing: Forgetting the past and looking forward to what lies ahead" (TLB). This verse assures us that "wholeness, completeness, or becoming what you should be" is in front of you and not behind you. Paul understood that trying to resolve your past keeps you from reaching into your future. Paul understood that the past never wants to stay the past, it wants to stay in the present in order to keep the past in the present. If the past can get you to "look back" or to "remember," you will then be trapped in either the turmoil or the tradition of your past.

But not only do you need to forget the hurts of the past, you also need to forget the helps of the past; not only the sadness, but also the success; not only the things that went wrong, but also the things that went right. Yesterday's problems or prosperities always want to stretch their tentacles into today's potentials for the purpose of disrupting or distorting. Yesterday's successes will trap you in the old and keep you from the new. Isaiah 43:18-19 states, "But the Lord says, 'Do not cling to events of the past or dwell on what happened long ago. Watch for the new thing I am going to do. It is happening already—you can see it now! I will make a path through the wilderness and give you streams of water there'" (TEV).

In the book of Exodus, God led the children of Israel out of Egypt. As He led them, they came up against an obstacle, the Red Sea. As they looked to God, He provided a way through the Red Sea. That was how God worked in their yesterdays, but it wasn't how He wanted to work in their todays. The old way was to provide dry land in the midst of the waters. The new was to provide water in the midst of the dry land.

Another example of this can be found in 2 Chronicles 20:12-22. In verse 12, King Jehoshaphat told the Lord, "We are powerless before this great multitude who are coming against us; nor do we know what to do, but our eyes are on Thee." This statement isn't entirely true, for if you read chapter 17, you will see that King Jehoshaphat had an army of 1,160,000 valiant warriors just in Jerusalem. This didn't even include all the warriors he had placed in fortified cities throughout the land of Judah. In the past, God had used this army to defeat many of the king's enemies. However, in chapter 20, a new enemy had appeared, but fortunately, Jehoshaphat knew better than to depend on the successes of yesterday. He didn't presume that just because God had helped him yesterday that He would do the same today. He knew the battle was not his but the Lord's, that it didn't matter how big his army was, because if God wasn't involved, they were doomed to fail. He knew that the power for victory didn't come from his military, but it came from his Messiah. Because he did not depend on the old, God did something new. Instead of defeating this enemy with a sword, the Lord used a song.

In Isaiah 33:21 God says, "But there the majestic One, the Lord, shall be for us. A place of rivers and wide canals, on which no boat with oars shall go." The place where the majestic One is—the place where He is there for us—is a place on which no boat with oars is allowed. In this place, no human effort is permitted. What God did yesterday becomes an oar, when we try to use it today. Yesterday's success was a result of God's power moving us from defeat to victory, from hurt to healing, and from bondage to liberty. God won't allow us to use what He did yesterday as an oar to get somewhere today. This place where the majestic One is, is a place where you forget about what you can do, and give yourself to the river of what He can do. It's a place where you forget about what you have, and give yourself to the river of what He has. It's a place where you forget about the old and give yourself to the river of the new. It's a place where you forget about what happened yesterday and give yourself to the river of what He wants to do today.

Both our Lord Jesus and Paul the Apostle told us not to "look back." This is the rule. Only when the Holy Spirit leads otherwise are you to move into the exception. Since the enemy wants you to "look back" while the Lord wants you to "look forward," it's going to be a battle to resist the enemy and obey the Lord. Paul said that he "brings all his energies to bear on this one thing: forgetting the past and looking forward to what lies ahead" (Philippians 3:13 TLB). It is a battle to quit looking backward, so you can start looking forward—and it is a daily battle. Though this battle will be difficult, with God's help, it possible.

WHAT TO DO WITH THE GARBAGE?

Each of us have problems in our past that continue to impede our progress in the present. The question is: What do you do when the garbage of your past begins to chase you? Let me answer that by using a story in the Old Testament, which proves that there is something in front of you God wants to lead you into which will deal with what's behind you.

God answered the above question in the story of the children of Israel coming out of Egypt in Exodus 14:1-15. The children of Israel were enslaved in Egypt and as a result of their slavery, they endured heartache and hardship for 400 years. God raised up Moses to deliver them out of their slavery and into His service. Egypt represented and contained all the hurts, failures, and regrets of their past. Moses came to deliver them from their past by leading them into God's future. From this story, you will learn that you break free from the struggles of the past by burying them in the successes of the future. For every Egyptian (a bondage of your past) that chases you, God has a Red Sea where He will bury them *if* you keep moving forward in your faith.

The first thing I want to point out is that it is God who stirs up the problems and pains of your past which then begin to plague your present. Exodus 14:4 states, "Once again I will harden Pharaoh's heart, and he [your past] will chase after you. I have planned this so I will receive great glory at the expense of Pharaoh and his armies" (TLB). God will use the gloom of your past to bring glory to your present. Only God knows when you are strong or mature enough to deal with some aspect of your past. Ecclesiastes 3:1 tells us that there "is an appointed time for every event under heaven," so if something from your past has surfaced and is causing you problems, please know that God is the one who allowed it to surface. He knows you are now ready to deal with it.

THE FIVE THINGS

Exodus 14:13-16 tells us five things we need to do when our past begins to chase us.

> But Moses said to the people, "Do not fear! Stand your ground and see the salvation of the Lord which He will accomplish for you today; for the Egyptians whom you have seen today, you will never see them again forever. The Lord will fight for you while you keep silent. Then the Lord said to Moses, "Why are you crying out to Me? Tell the sons of Israel to go forward."

From this passage, you learn that the first thing you need to do is "stand your ground." The Hebrew word for *stand* is *yatsab*, which means *to take a stand and set yourself against something or someone that is seeking to take from you.* In other words, don't let something from your past cause you to lose the ground God has already given you.

First Chronicles 11:12-14 tells the story of one of David's mighty men who took his stand in the midst of a field the Lord had given to the army of David for food. This mighty man, in the face of overwhelming odds, took his stand and refused to allow the Philistines to take what God had given. What gave this mighty man the faith to believe that God would help him keep this field was the fact that God is the one who had given it to them. God will always empower you to keep what He has given to you.

The second thing that you need to do is "see the salvation of the Lord." The Hebrew word for see is *ra-ah*, which means to *give attention to, to observe, to learn from, to behold, and to look intently at.* It implies that God wants to use the enemies of your past to teach you the lessons you will need for the future. He will use your failures to teach you to be successful, and He will use your hurts in such a way that they will become helps. God will use the past to equip you for His purpose.

Isaiah 53:5 states, "By His stripes we are healed." The Lord's wounds on the cross heal us, and in a similar fashion, our stripes also give us the authority for healing. In the very place the enemy wounds us, once we are healed, we are given the power to heal others. The Lord allows bad things to happen to His people, so they can receive the compassion for others through which the power of healing operates. Every bad thing that happens to us bestows on us the authority to do good. The New Testament equivalent of this principle is found in Hebrews 12:2: "Let us keep our eyes fixed on Jesus, on whom our faith depends from beginning to end." The Greek word for *fix* is *aforaoo* which means *to turn the eyes away from other things and fix them on something else.* It means to quit looking at your hurts, and start looking at the Healer; quit looking at what you don't have, and start looking at Whom you do have; and it means to quit looking at the mistakes, and start looking at the Messiah.

The third thing you need to do is found in the phrase

"the Lord will fight for you while you keep silent" Another way of saying this is "stay silent." Talking will cause you to reason away the supernatural with the natural. Reasoning will make you adjust what God has said to fit the facts of your situation. On the other hand, faith will make you adjust the facts of your situation to fit what God has said. The facts of this story are that God had delivered the children of Israel out of Egypt to the Red Sea. He then hardened Pharaoh's heart so he would chase after them. With no escape in front of them, they began to reason and declare that God had somehow deceived them. Exodus 14:10-11 tells us,

> "And as Pharaoh drew near, the sons of Israel looked, and behold, the Egyptians were marching after them, and they became very frightened; so the sons of Israel cried out to the Lord. Then they said to Moses, is it because there were no graves in Egypt that you have taken us away to die in the wilderness. Why have you dealt with us in this way, bringing us out of Egypt."

God said He would engage their enemies if they would disengage their mouth. This is supported by Proverbs 18:21 which tells us, "What you say can preserve life or destroy it." You need to quit breathing life into the problems of your past by talking about them. Instead of talking about what is behind you, stay silent and start listening to the One who is in front of you. Shut up and God will fight for you. When you quit talking, complaining, accusing, blaming, and gossiping, then God starts fighting. Isaiah 30:15-16 states, "The Sovereign Lord, the Holy One of Israel, says, Only in returning to me and waiting for me will you be saved. In quietness and confidence is your strength."

The fourth thing you need to do is described by the phrase "stop crying." The Hebrew word translated *cry* in verse 15 is *tsa-aq,* which means: *"to make a loud cry for the purpose of drawing attention."* Galatians 5:24 states, "Those who are Christ's have crucified the flesh with its passions and desires." God doesn't want to heal your flesh; He wants to crucify it. A lot of the therapeutic counseling Christians go through is an attempt to heal what God is trying to kill. The problem isn't that someone hurt your feelings, the problem is that your feelings always get hurt. You live in a fallen world, where both saved and unsaved people deal with a fallen nature. It is not God's purpose to protect you from this world, but to use it to produce in you the ability to prosper in spite of it.

In 1980, when I was released from prison after eight years, I traveled from Florida to Pennsylvania to see my father to try and reconcile our relationship. However, because of the kind of son I was prior to becoming a Christian, my father refused to see me. After I told him I traveled more than 1,000 miles to see him, he relented and agreed to meet me in a bar. When he came into the bar, he proceeded to tell me how much he hated me and all the reasons why he no longer considered me his son—and then stormed out. In my flesh, I was hurt and everything in me wanted to give up, go back to Florida, and never expose myself to that kind of pain again.

But in my spirit, I was understanding. Instead of re-acting to the pain my earthly father was inflicting, I decided to react to the love that my heavenly Father was dispensing. Instead of sowing to the flesh by giving in to the pain, I de-cided to sow to the Spirit by giving in to the love. I couldn't allow how my dad was as a father determine how I was go-ing to be as a son. Therefore, each year I would go back and try to reconcile with my father, and each year the same sce-nario would play out. But in the seventh year, God changed my father's heart, and he re-embraced me as his son. Instead of getting counseling for the pain, I endured. I decided to commit myself to the process of sowing to the Spirit, instead of the flesh, and "in due season I was able to reap."

The fifth and final thing you need to do is found in the phrase "start moving forward." Moving forward will bring you into those things which will enable you to deal with what is behind you. Moving forward will not resolve your past, but it will reconcile (change) your life. Colossians 1:20 states, "God through Jesus will reconcile all things to Himself." The Greek word for *reconcile* is *apokatallasso* which *means to change from one condition to another*. It means that as you move forward in your faith, God will change your hurts into health; He will change your problems into potentials; and He will change your stumbling blocks into steppingstones.

Remember, Christian maturity happens when you move out of your past into God's breathtaking future. The past cannot be changed, but your response to it can be. The past is valuable as a guidepost, but dangerous if used as a hitching post.

EIGHT

THORNS THAT HELP

God's way of using our weakness to produce His strength

In the last several years, God has been restoring a truth to the Church. This particular truth had lost some of its power because of the church's familiarity with it. Once we become too familiar with something, all too often we begin to take it for granted. Once something is taken for granted, it loses the power to significantly impact one's life. The truth that God is restoring to the Church is the truth of His grace. He has been restoring this truth by having several prominent writers focus on this important and powerful concept. Chuck Swindoll began this restoration by writing a book called *The Great Grace Awakening.* Philip Yancey wrote a book titled *What Is So Wonderful About Grace.* John Piper wrote a book titled *Future Grace.* And finally, Max Lucado wrote a book *In the Grip of His Grace.* These are just a few of the books God has stirred people to write in order to bring us back to and help us rediscover this very powerful truth from God's Word.

If we are going to talk about grace, however, then we

have to talk about another truth that goes with it, and that truth is mercy. Mercy and grace are two sides of the same coin, two halves of one truth. In order to talk about one, we have to talk about the other. A very simple definition for mercy would be *not getting what you deserve*. I am grateful that on July 26, 1972, God didn't give me what I deserved.

As you know from chapter one, I had just taken the life of another human being. I deserved to have my life taken, but God was merciful towards me and instead of receiving death, I received the gift of eternal life. I want you to know that I am just as grateful that God did not give me what I deserved as a result of the life I lived yesterday. Some of the thoughts I thought, some of the attitudes I demonstrated, and some of the actions I took deserved some kind of retribution. But again, God was merciful towards me. The Bible says in First Chronicles 16:34 that "God is good; for His mercy endureth forever." The reason it will last forever is because mercy is something that we will always need. Lamentations 3:22-23 tells us that "His mercies are new every morning."

Knowing that I need new mercies every day is what motivates me to get out of bed for my quiet time so I can avail myself of His mercy. A very simple definition for grace would be "getting something you don't deserve." The combination of not getting what I deserved, and then getting something I didn't deserve makes these combined truths quite powerful. Mercy causes God not to treat us as our sins deserve, while grace causes God to treat us as His Son deserves.

One of the ways that I try to communicate this truth to the inmates to whom I minister is by going up to the biggest and strongest inmate in my class and asking him to stand up. Because of his size, he is towering over me. I then turn to the other inmates and ask them, "What do you think would happen if I turned around and smacked this guy right in the face and called him a derogatory name?" Immediately the other inmates start yelling, "He will stomp you." I then ask if I would deserve to be stomped, and they all agree I would.

Then I say, "Let's say this man understands both the mercy and grace of God. Therefore, he allows God's mercy to restrain his anger towards my offence and he doesn't stomp me. Then, he allows God's grace to release his love for me the offender, and he pulls out a $50 bill and gives it to me. First, he didn't give me what I deserved, and second, he gave me something I didn't deserve." Then I ask them if that scenario actually happened, how many of them would get in line to slap this man, and they all raise their hands. The reason they respond like that is because mercy and grace are a good deal. Since it is such a good deal, I want to explore this concept more deeply so you too can be revived in your understanding, and therefore get in on the good deals that His mercy and grace afford you.

To do so, I want to examine several places in Scripture that will help awaken you to this wonderful truth of *grace*. In 2 Corinthians 12:1-6, Paul wrote about an experience he once had. This experience was so unbelievable that he couldn't bring himself to talk about it in the first person: "I know a man in Christ who fourteen years ago . . . was caught up to the third heaven . . . and heard things so astounding that they are beyond a man's power to describe or put in words." As a result of this experience, he made these comments in verse 7: "Because of the surpassing greatness of these revelations, to keep me from exalting myself."

Here Paul identified a problem we all face when God begins to give or do something significant in our lives. The problem is that when God gives or does something, we have a tendency to start leaning on what He does or gives and stop leaning on the One who is giving or doing. We start leaning on the revelations, instead of the Revelator; the things of God, instead of the God of the things; or the gifts of God, instead of the Giver of the gifts.

The problem here is a "me" problem. The solution is found in the last part of verse 7: "There was given me a thorn in the flesh, a messenger of Satan to buffet me." You need to understand the one who gave the thorn was the one who loved Paul the most. This was a thorn designed to help Paul, not hurt him. But make no mistake, it was still a thorn. It was sharp, and when stuck with it, it caused pain. To make matters worse, God placed this thorn in the hands of someone from the enemy's camp, "a messenger of Satan." There is a logical reason why God does this.

Let's say if God was to give me a thorn with which to stick my wife in order to cause her to be more dependent on Him. My love for her would make it difficult for me to actually stick her. I might show it to her, and even threaten her with it, but when push came to shove, my love for her would keep me from sticking her. Somebody from the enemy's camp, however, doesn't have that problem. In the Old Testament, when God wanted to make adjustments in His people, He would always hand them over to their enemies for a season. He did this to help them, not hurt them—though some hurt was involved. It's important we don't focus on the one who holds the thorn, but the One who gave it to them to hold.

One of the things all Christians need to understand is that the devil is God's devil. Psalm 119:91 states, "For all things are Thy servants." Therefore, Satan is God's servant. If you are a born-again believer in Jesus Christ, Satan has to get permission from God to do anything to you. We can see this in the book of Job when Satan was given permission to afflict Job. We can also see this truth in Luke 22:31 when Satan asked permission of Jesus to sift Peter as wheat is sifted. Everything the enemy does, God can use to serve His purpose. The weapons Satan uses to hurt us, God can use as tools to help us; the things he would use to tear us down, God can use to build us up; and the things he would use as stumbling blocks, God can use as steppingstones.

In Job's affliction, God was glorified and Job was abundantly blessed. In the midst of being sifted, Peter had something addressed and transformed in him which equipped him to be a strength to his brothers. Romans 8:28 states, "We know that God causes all things to work together for good to those who love God, to those who are called according to His purpose." This verse doesn't say that all things are good, it says God is at work for good in all things.

Paul understood that thorns given by God are "thorns that help." Paul went on to write in 2 Corinthians 12:8-9, "Concerning this [thorn] I entreated the Lord three times that it might depart from me. And He has said to me, 'My grace is sufficient for you, for power is perfected in weakness.'" Thorns help us by making us aware once again of our need for God. Thorns make us aware of what we can't do, so we will press into the One who can do anything; they make us aware of what we don't have, so we will press into the One who has everything; and they make us aware of what we don't know, so we will press into the One who knows all things. Thorns make us weak so we will seek His strength; thorns make us aware of our need so we will seek His provision; they make us empty so we will seek His fulness; and they make us helpless so we will seek His power. It's in our place of weakness that God gains access to our lives, so therefore thorns in the flesh result in power in the Spirit.

I have learned over the years that God blessing my outward life can contribute to the undoing of my spiritual life for God. I have found that blessedness can be one of the greatest spiritual perils because it has a tendency of dulling my keen sense of dependency on God. I am most susceptible to this peril right after I have experienced a spiritual success or right after I have done an exploit for God. Those are the times when I am most inclined to hold a wrong, dangerous, and over-inflated view of my strengths.

Paul gets so excited about this revelation that in verses 9 and 10, he begins to rejoice in anything that made him aware of what he didn't have so he would press into what God had:

> Now I am glad to boast about how weak I am; I am glad to be a living demonstration of Christ's power, instead of showing off my own power and abilities. Since I know it is all for Christ's good, I am quite happy about the thorn, and about insults and hardships, persecutions and difficulties; for when I am weak, then I am strong, the less I have, the more I depend on him.

Read how the translation called *The Message* renders these verses:

> Because of the extravagance of those revelations,

and so I wouldn't get a big head, I was given the gift of a handicap to keep me in constant touch with my limitations. Satan's angel did his best to get me down; what he in fact did was push me to my knees. No danger then of walking around high and mighty! At first, I didn't think of it as a gift, and begged God to remove it. Three times I did that, and then He told me, "My grace is enough; it's all you need. My strength comes into its own in your weakness." Once I heard that, I was glad to let it happen, I quit focusing on the handicap and began appreciating the gift. It was a case of Christ's strength moving in on my weakness. Now I take limitations in stride, and with good cheer, these limitations that cut me down to size, abuse, accidents, opposition, bad breaks, I just let Christ take over. And so the weaker I am the stronger I become.

THE RIGHT MATH

You need to make sure that in dealing with God you don't use the wrong math. The wrong math explains it like this:

your abilities + your experiences + your training + your personality + your appearance + your past + the expectations of others = what you can do.

The Lord specializes in working through ordinary people who believe in an extraordinary God who will do His work through them. His equation looks like this:

your willingness + your weakness + His will + His supernatural power = great works of God.

Helplessness, weakness, need, and emptiness are good places to be in, for our dependency on God is just another word for power. This is why it's important to remember that thorns in the flesh translate into power in the Spirit.

Jesus said in Matthew 5:3, "Blessed are the poor in spirit, for theirs is the kingdom of heaven." This is the first of the Beatitudes and serves as the introduction to Jesus' Sermon on the Mount. In Scripture first things are important because they tend to be foundational in nature. A foundation is what you build on; it's what anchors everything else. Jesus chose this first Beatitude to be the stone on which He was to build His entire sermon. With that in mind, let's examine it in that context. I am spending some time here because many people just skim over this verse. The reason they do so is because it uses a word that makes us uncomfortable. The word is *poor.*

Christians don't like this word especially those of us in Western civilization. We've been taught all our lives that poverty is to be avoided at all costs, that being poor is wrong and is a curse from the devil. As a result, much of our Christianity is saturated with the idea is that the ultimate blessing of God is for us to become wealthy. The idea of this first Beatitude is that we need to be poor enough to receive. The characteristic of poverty that God wants to bless us with is being aware of what we don't have, don't know, and can't do so we will press into His Kingdom where He does have, does know, and can do. What keeps many of us from receiving from God is our sense of being rich instead of being poor. Revelations 3:17 brings this point out very clearly: "Because you say, 'I am rich, and have become wealthy, and have need of nothing,' and you do not know that you are wretched and miserable and poor and blind and naked."

The *Berean Translation* renders Matthew 5:3 this way: "Blessed are those who sense spiritual poverty for the kingdom of God is theirs." As a result of meditating on this verse, I realized that poverty is what opens up the kingdom of God to us. Even though God has blessed us a lot, we must find a way to maintain a sense of spiritual poverty in the midst of our abundant blessings. Self-sufficiency in any area of your life will hinder you from the ongoing riches of the Kingdom. The windows of heaven open when you plead for help; when you run out of options; when you stop demanding justice and start pleading for mercy; when you stop bragging and start begging.

Recently I went through a season where I began to evaluate my Christian experience. And though I am older in the Lord and have more knowledge, I didn't feel as close to Him as I have in the past, especially in the early days of my walk with Him. It dawned on me that the blessing of my natural life had contributed to the undoing of my spiritual life. When I first got saved, I was poverty-stricken in every area of my life which caused me to depend totally on Him. However, now that I'm thirty years down the road and God has enriched me in every way, I don't seek Him as much because I don't need Him as much.

NO FORMULA, JUST GOD

In July of 1986, I started the church in Orlando, Florida, primarily to give ongoing pastoral care to people who were coming out of prison. Within three years we went from four people to about 150 people. Soon after starting the church, a couple who was attending called up and asked if they could come in for some marital counseling. They told me they had been married for ten years and if some things didn't change, they were headed for divorce. I had a problem in that I was poverty stricken in the area of marital counseling. I had only been married for a couple of years and up until that time hadn't had any real marital problems. Because of my poverty of not knowing what to say or do, I pressed into the One who knows all things and can do anything.

Their appointment was for 11:00 a.m. I got to my office at 8:00 a.m. where I prayed desperately for three hours. During that time, God quickened a Scripture to me out of Proverbs. As I meditated on this verse, I sensed God wanted me to go in like Rambo and take a very militant approach to applying this verse to this couple's marriage. The couple arrived at 11:00 and for the next two hours we battled it out. Every time they raised an excuse for not changing, I would direct them to this verse and said, "No, that doesn't matter. What matters is what God says." Fortunately, in the midst of this counseling session God's grace and revelation broke in on their understanding which produced repentance and reconciliation. Because I was poor in the area of marital counseling, I was able to receive the riches of God's kingdom for this couple.

But I now had a problem. I had become to a degree rich in the area of marital counseling so much so that the next time a couple came for marital counseling, I thought I knew exactly what they needed. Instead of arriving three hours before the appointment to pray for God's intervention and direction, I arrived just a few minutes before our meeting and asked God to bless as He did the last time. I used the same Scripture from Proverbs and applied in the same military way. Unfortunately, instead of helping this couple, it hurt them. Within a half hour they were gone, never to attend our church again. I heard later that they had divorced.

What went wrong is that I was no longer poor enough to receive. Instead of pressing into God's knowledge, I pressed into mine; instead of looking to God for a new experience, I pressed into my old experience. If I had sought God out of my poverty, He may have quickened the same scripture, but because this couple was different than the previous couple, He may have guided me to go in like Forrest Gump and apply it in a very gentile way. I have found that as God allows me to progress in my Christian walk, there is a danger of relegating Him to a smaller and smaller place. I have found that it is easy to do the stuff God has trained me to do and then leave Him out of it when I go to do it. Now I am not saying that God can't use our knowledge, our training, or our experience. What I am saying is that I have to approach each situation with a sense of poverty and then leave it up to God as to whether He will draw from what He has already imparted to me or give and teach me something new.

We can see this dynamic in the story of Uzziah who was made king in the place of his father Amaziah as told in 2 Chronicles 26. The first verse says, "And all the people of Judah took Uzziah, who was sixteen years old, and made him king in the place of his father Amaziah." Would you agree with me that at sixteen years of age, Uzziah was poverty stricken in all areas of what it took to be a king? At his age he was still developing physically, he probably had never been in battle, and he was unproven in the ways of leading a nation. Fortunately for him, he allowed his poverty to cause him to press into God's riches.

Verse five states, "And he continued to seek God in the days of Zechariah, who had understanding through the vision of God; and as long as he sought the LORD, God prospered him." What caused him to seek the Lord was the fact that he didn't have, didn't know, and couldn't do. As long as he sought the Lord, his poverty made way for God's prosperity. Unfortunately, something happened in verse 15. Because 2 Chronicles is a historical book, though we have only progressed through ten verses, a lot happened since verse five. Uzziah was no longer sixteen but had reached the age of thirty. He was fully developed physically, had been in many battles, and led the nation into many victories as God prospered and blessed him. Because of his many successes he had lost his sense of poverty for we learn in verse 15, "And in Jerusalem he made engines of war invented by skillful men to be on the towers and on the corners, for the purpose of shooting arrows and great stones. Hence his fame spread afar, *for he was marvelously helped until he was strong"* (emphasis added)

Do you see that God had marvelously helped him until he became strong? Somewhere in the midst of God prospering Uzziah, he began depending on the strength that had been given to him instead of the strength that he had sought from God. Somewhere along the way he thought it was his strength instead of God's. Verse 16 goes on to say out of the *Darby Translation*, "But when he became strong his heart was lifted up to [his] own downfall. *The Message* says it this way: "But then the strength and success went to his head. Arrogant and proud, he fell." And the *New Living Translation* interprets it this way: "But when he had become powerful, he also became proud, which led to his downfall."

ONE PLAYER OR TWO?

Because of the ministry that God has called me to, I travel a lot. When I travel, I used to always try and get my two children a gift to help take the sting out of me being gone so often. Being a good Dad, I always tried to get a gift that was both educational and entertaining. Because we are a very computer literate family, I normally got them a computer game that met this criterion. Years ago I came home from a trip and when I got home my daughter Jessica, who was thirteen at the time, had a friend over by the name of

Amber. After we greeted one another, Jessica asked me if I had gotten her a gift. I told her that since she was taking tennis lessons at school, I had bought her a computer game that would teach her the fundamentals of tennis. As I sat down to go through my mail, she and her friend loaded the game on my computer since it was the most powerful one in the house.

After a few minutes of playing, I heard my daughter groan. As I looked up, I saw the source of her groaning was the fact that her friend Amber was beating her at this game of tennis again and again. Almost every one of her serves was an ace and no matter where Jessica hit the ball, Amber got to it and volleyed back with a great shot. I asked Amber if she had played this game before and she said no. I then asked if she plays tennis on a real court and again, she said no. By this time, I was frustrated for my daughter, so I decided to coach my daughter. I watched how Amber used her control stick and coached Jessica to do it the same way. But still no matter what we did, Amber won every time. I couldn't figure out how she could be so much better than Jessica and I since this was her first time playing the game.

Then it dawned on me that when they loaded the game onto the computer, they never switched it from one player to two players. Jessica wasn't playing Amber; she was playing the computer so no matter what she did with her controller, the ball was going to go where the computer wanted it to go. In essence this what happened to Uzziah when out of his weaknesses, he sought God's strength. At sixteen when he first went into battle, young, unskilled, and unproven, God helped him. It didn't matter what he did with his sword, God like the computer was directing him to do what He wanted done, which caused the king to be victorious and prosper in his kingdom.

Somewhere along the way, however, Uzziah began to think he was achieving his success instead of the Lord, which caused his heart to be lifted up and his life to be dragged down. Like all of us, Uzziah needed to learn how to maintain a sense of spiritual poverty in the midst of an abundant blessing.

I don't want God to remove His abundant blessing from my life, just my dependency upon it. However, if for some reason I can't do that, it's my prayer that God will do for me what he did for Paul. Remember, what Paul wrote in 2 Corinthians 12:8: ". . . that the thorn was given to him to keep him from exalting himself." I am grateful God loves me enough that when I start leaning on the revelations instead of the revelator, he will give me a thorn to help me exalt His strength and not my own.

NINE

DESIRING GOD'S JUDGMENTS INSTEAD OF DREADING THEM

God's way of using His judgment to produce His righteousness in our lives

First Peter 4:17 states, "For it is time for judgment to begin with the household of God" (NASB). I have always feared the words "judgment of God." Even though I was not raised in a Christian home, I heard my parents and others attribute the great calamities and disasters that happened in the world to the "judgment of God." I got the impression that God was angry at most people because they weren't perfect, and in what some would call "His righteous indignation" would let a plane crash, or let a hurricane or a tornado come through an area, or unleash a new disease like AIDS into the world. Since I wasn't perfect, then it was just a matter of time before the "judgment of God" was going to come upon my life. Instead of this becoming a deterrent to sin in my life, however, it became a driving force to sin even more. This was because I had no hope of ever being perfect, thus escaping the "judgment of God," I then adopted the life philosophy of "let's eat, drink and be merry for tomorrow we die."

Not only did I have to worry about God judging my many imperfections, I also discovered that His creation, namely mankind, was just as prone to judge. Throughout my life, I learned that weaknesses wouldn't be tolerated and imperfections brought consequences. When I was a child growing up, I was judged too small, so I didn't make the basketball team. In baseball, I was judged not good enough, so I played right field and batted last. In my teen years, I was judged too rowdy so parents wouldn't let their kids associate with me. My own parents judged me more capable than I was, which brought about unrealistic expectations.

In school, I was judged too rebellious, so I was expelled. When I joined the military, I was judged unable to change so I was undesirably discharged. My family judged me as too bothersome, so they turned their backs on me. Society judged me too violent, so I was sent to prison. All of these judgments were righteous and true, but they weren't implemented to help me, but rather to hurt me—not to change me, but to condemn me.

From the moment I met Jesus, however, I discovered His judgments were totally different than what I thought they would be. Not only are they different than man's judgments, they are higher than man's judgments. Where man's judgments are punitive in nature, God's are redemptive. Man's judgments are designed to condemn what is wrong in man, God's judgments are designed to bring forth what is right in man. Man's judgments are meant to condemn us for where we are at, God's judgments will bring us to where we should be. Man's judgments are designed to punish man's problems, God's judgments are designed to develop man's potential. When man judges, we get hurt, but when God judges we get help.

Therefore, God's judgments are to be desired, not dreaded; embraced, not rejected; to be run towards, not run from. The writers of the Bible had this perspective when they wrote of God's judgment. When they spoke of the "judgment of God," they encouraged us to seek it, to follow after it, and to get in on it whenever we could. They talked about rewards and benefits that His judgments were meant to bring us. Psalm 19:9-12 is a good example of what I am talking about:

> The judgments of the Lord are true; they are righteous altogether. They are more desirable than gold, yes, than much fine gold; sweeter also than honey and the drippings of the honeycomb. Moreover, by them Thy servant is warned; In keeping them there is great reward (NASB).

This passage indicates that the judgments of God are true, righteous, desirable, valuable, sweet, and full of rewards. Those all sound like positive traits to me. When God judges you, you should be able to say, "Man, that was sweet" or "Gold couldn't do for me what that did for me." As I mentioned in previous chapters, in 1972 at the age of 22, I was sentenced by a Florida judge to 30 years in prison. At the time, I thought this was the worst thing that could have ever happened to me. Little did I know it was going to turn out to be one of the best things that could ever have happened to me. I went into prison as a cheater of society, I came out a champion for society. I went in as one who hurts others, I came out as one who helps people. I went in a prisoner, I came out a preacher. I went in full of sin, I came out full of the Son.

In verse 11, the Hebrew word for *warned* is *zahar*, whose primary meaning isn't *warned* but *to be taught by receiving the light of God*. The PBV translation renders this verse as follows: "by them [the judgments] thy servant is taught." Then Helen Spurrell, a noted Hebrew scholar, *The Translation Of the Old Testament Scriptures From The Original Hebrew* (Helen Spurrell, *The Bible from 26 Translations*, page 996) puts it this way: "by them thy servant is enlightened." And the *Amplified Version* brings even more clarity to the meaning: "moreover, by them is Your servant warned (reminded, illuminated, and instructed)." The idea is that God's judgments carry His revelation for our lives. In other words, God teaches us by judging us. My eight years in prison afforded me an education no amount of money could buy. Sumter Correctional Institution became Sumter Bible College for me. This book is a result of all the revelation those eight years of judgment brought to me.

MY PRISON JUDGMENT

Not only has it brought me riches, it has also brought the promised sweetness to my life. Noah *Webster's 1828 Dictionary* used these adjectives to describe something sweet: "agreeable, pleasing, fresh, mild, soft, gentle, with the idea of causing one to be grateful." I'm sure you have heard the expression "a hardened con[vict]" because that is what happens to some people who have been in prison. For most inmates, prison makes them bitter, not better; it makes them troubled, not triumphant; and it makes them hard, not happy. Because I realized God's justice is filtered through God's mercy, however, I knew the intended purpose for the judgment of my life was to impart His righteousness to my life. Therefore, prison became for me a means whereby I was changed for the better.

It was in prison where I learned that happiness doesn't depend on the condition of your circumstances, but on the condition of your heart. I went into prison a disagreeable, repugnant, sour, harsh, hard, and rough person who had caused everyone I knew to regret they ever knew me. I came out of prison an agreeable, pleasing, fresh, mild, soft, and gentle person who is now causing everyone I meet to be grateful I'm in their lives. God's judgment of my life in those eight years was one of the sweetest things that has ever happened to me.

The purpose of God's judgment is not immediately apparent because God puts the peaceable fruit of righteousness for our lives in the midst of the discipline of our lives (see Hebrews 12:11). In Luke 22:31-32, God put the converting of Peter's soul in the midst of the sifting of his life. Throughout the Scriptures, God has placed some of His best stuff in what the world would consider some of the worst containers. In the Old Testament, God used slavery and prison to bring Joseph into the palace of Pharaoh where he was in position to save his family. God used 40 years of exile to prepare Moses to lead His people out of slavery. God used 40 years of wandering around a wilderness to transform a nation of slaves into a nation of kings.

In the New Testament, we learn that God uses tribulation to produce perseverance, character, and hope in our lives (see Romans 5:3-4). God uses afflictions to produce in us His glory (see 2 Corinthians 4:17). Furthermore, God uses trials to bring us into perfection where we lack nothing (see James 1:2). There is an edge to God's judgment that has a way of initially making us think He is out to punish us instead of promoting us. That was certainly true in the life of Genesis Joseph.

It is for this reason that the psalmist in Psalm 19:11 states concerning the judgments that "in keeping them there is great reward." The Hebrew word for *in keeping them* is *shamar*, which is defined as *waiting and watching for the purpose of observing.* The idea is that when God brings a judgment into your life, you need to wait and watch for the teaching, instruction, and guidance God wants to bring to you, which will then add great value to your life. The translation called *The Message* renders the latter part of verse eleven this way: "His judgments will direct us to hidden treasure." Isaiah 45:3 in the *Living Translation* corroborates this when it states, "and I will give you treasures hidden in the darkness." God's judgments can be dark, but they contain a treasure, and if we wait, watch and observe, we will discover great riches for our lives.

SCATTERHEAD

Let me share a great treasure I discovered in the midst of some extreme darkness. The prison I was in was one of the worst in the state of Florida. Inmates called it "gladiator school" because you had to learn to fight or fall prey to all the predators who lived there. This prison averaged about 230 assaults, one inmate upon another, every year I was there. A lot of these assaults were sexual in nature. Because of God's favor on my life, my first couple of years in prison were incident free. I learned that inmates respected strength, whether it was physical strength, mental strength, or emotional strength. Because of my strength of faith and will, I gained the respect of most inmates. However, three years after I was in, I was transferred to the outside warehouse to work as a clerk.

One of the men who worked there loading trucks took a sexual interest in me. This man was an African American, six feet eight inches tall, and his muscles had muscles. Because of a certain mental disorder he had, the other inmates called him Scatterhead. Every day in front of others, he would make remarks about what he would do to me sexually if he ever caught me in the back of the warehouse by myself, and it was just a matter of time before he made me his sexual partner. I was embarrassed by what he said, and fearful that he would follow through with his remarks. I didn't know why God was allowing this to happen but I knew He loved me, and was at work for good for my life.

I also knew that Satan's temptations could be used by God as His testings. I knew that Satan tempts us in order to bring out the worst in us, but that God tests us in order to bring out the best in us. Whether the worst or the best comes out depends on how we respond to the things God has allowed into our lives. I knew God had allowed Scatterhead to come into my life, so I was determined that the best was going to come out of me. After praying, I decided to respond to him the way Luke 6:27-30 says I should:

> "To you who are ready for the truth, I say this: Love your enemies. Let them bring out the best in you, not the worst. When someone gives you a hard time, respond with the energies of prayer for that person. If someone slaps you in the face, stand there and take it. If someone grabs your shirt, gift wrap your best coat and make a present of it. If someone takes unfair advantage of you, use the occasion to practice the servant life. No more tit-for-tat stuff. Live generously" (MSG).

Therefore, I prayed for Scatterhead every day, and I looked for ways to bless him. One of his duties was to sweep the warehouse and clean the bathrooms, so at least once a week, I would take care of these duties for him. Instead of things getting better, however, they got worse. He took my kindness as weakness, which only encouraged him to be even more vulgar than he was before. After weeks of this, I was praying and telling God I couldn't endure much more abuse, and I sensed God tell me that He wanted me to stand up to Scatterhead. Though Scatterhead was bigger and stronger, I had a confidence and faith that God was going to help me like He had helped David with Goliath.

I immediately left my desk where I was praying, went to the warehouse and informed Scatterhead I was no longer going to take what he was saying. He responded that we could settle this right now in the back of the warehouse. Confident God was with me, I said, "Let's go." We went to the back of the warehouse, and with the other inmates who worked there looking on, we squared off. I threw the first punch, thinking God was going to anoint my fist like He did David's sling, and I was going to slay this giant. Much to my surprise, my fist got more hurt than his face. All my feeble attempt did was make this already angry man even angrier.

He proceeded to pick me up and body slam me onto the concrete, and then in a rage, he spewed profanities at me while he kept punching me and kicking me. I was being beat so bad that I kept thinking if he didn't stop, I was going to die. Deep inside me I cried out and said, "Lord, help me." The moment I said that, Scatterhead stopped. The moment he stopped, I felt the anointing of God come on me with power and authority. I slowly got to my feet, and then told all the other inmates to leave us alone and they left. Weakened and bloody, I told Scatterhead to sit down, and he did. Then I looked at him and said that ever since I had come to the warehouse, I tried to get him to respect who I was, and what I believed in, but that the only thing he respected was what we had just done.

I proceeded to tell him, with tears in my eyes, that if we had to go through this same thing every day, he was going to learn to respect me, or he was going to have to kill me. God so anointed those words that Scatterhead started crying and apologized to me, saying I didn't deserve any of the things he had said or done. Two days later, I had the privilege of leading him to the Lord. That day he went from being "Scatterhead," to being "Carey," which was his real name. I later discovered he was the way he was because he had been physically and sexually abused as a child and abandoned by his family. The treasures I found in the midst of this dark time in my life were exceeding.

Through this experience with Carey, I learned what it means to be "more than a conqueror." A victor is someone who defeats his enemy, a conqueror is someone who wins his enemy. I learned that people who deserve love the least need it the most. I learned that people who are the hardest on the outside are actually the softest on the inside. I learned that it is only hurting people who hurt others, and if you can somehow endure the pain they are afflicting while you seek to minister healing to their pain, then not only will they stop hurting, they will stop hurting others. And I learned that God will help you not to be overcome with evil while He instructs and empowers you to overcome evil with good (see Romans 12:21).

Does this mean that I want to get beat up again? Obviously, the answer is no, but if getting beat up will bring another Carey into the Kingdom of God, then I would gladly endure it. For God helped my physical wounds to heal, but Carey's eternal wounds would not have healed had not God intervened in his life by transforming an object of His contempt into an instrument of His conversion. Another good example that God's judgments should be desired and not dreaded is found in Isaiah 26:7-10, which states,

> "The way of the righteous is smooth; O Upright One, make the path of the righteous level. Indeed, while following the way of Thy judgments, O Lord, we have waited for Thee eagerly; Thy name, even Thy memory, is the desire of our souls. At night my soul longs for Thee, indeed, my spirit within me seeks Thee diligently; for when the earth experiences Thy judgments the inhabitants of the world learn righteousness. Though the wicked is

shown favor, he does not learn righteousness; he deals unjustly in the land of uprightness, and does not perceive the majesty of the Lord."

The writer stated that it's by following the way of judgments that our way becomes smooth, our path becomes level, we learn righteousness, we are shown favor, and encounter His majesty. The writer encouraged us to cry out for judgment because His judgments will bring up the valleys that we consistently fall into; and bring down the mountains that we constantly are running into. Because the righteous realized that God's righteousness, favor and majesty are found in the midst of His judgments, then they are not running from them, but are actually running after them.

Verse nine is especially important in understanding the dual nature of God's judgments. As we have already learned, there is a dark side to God's judgments, but there are also riches; there is suffering, but there is also glory. In this verse, Isaiah started out by saying *at night* and the Hebrew word for *night* is *laylah*, which is defined as *gloom or calamity.* The implication is that Isaiah was in the throes of some intense trials and his response was like the writer of James recommended: "Count it all joy when you fall into diverse trials" (James 1:2 NASB).

Isaiah longed for God, because he knew this judgment was bringing him closer to God, so he began to diligently seek for God by sifting through the darkness in order to find the treasures of His righteousness, favor, and majesty. Isaiah concluded this thought by saying that the wicked are shown the same favor of God's judgments but they don't see it as a means of teaching them something and thus miss out on His majesty. The Hebrew word for *favor* is *chanan,* which means *to have mercy on and be gracious towards.*

The implication is that God's judgments are one of His greatest sources of mercy and grace for our lives. All the people who I was in prison with were shown the same mercy and grace I was in that their lives and sins were judged right along with mine, but many didn't perceive the majesty of the Lord. They saw the judgments as God condemning their lives, instead of a means to conform to His life; they saw the judgments as a punishment of their sins, instead of a means of promotion into the Savior; and they saw the judgments as something that caused the loss of what they had, instead of seeing it as a means to gain all that He has.

As we have already seen, God will judge the sins of our lives in order to bring us His mercy and grace—which will then save our souls. One of the verses that brings real sobriety to my life is the one in Numbers 32:23 which states, "Your sin will find you out" (NASB). Either I acknowledge my sin or it will be acknowledged for me. Someone once said, "You are as sick as the secrets you keep." Confession is not telling God what we did for He already knows, but rather confession is simply agreeing with Him. He is the "all-seeing one." He knows perfectly and completely what we are. Once we acknowledge this, then all attempts at silence or secrecy seem juvenile and ridiculous.

Let me make one thing very clear, and that is our God hates sin but He loves sinners. We need to be aware of His holiness, which would condemn us; and of His Love, which esteems and redeems us. His holiness will keep us from being arrogant, and His love will keep us from being frightened. God's standards do not change, but neither does His compassion. We are naked before Him, in the same sense that a person is sprawled naked on the operating table before a surgeon. The person is neither boastful nor embarrassed, for he or she understands that his or her exposed condition is a necessity of their relationship. Whether the doctor finds good or evil, what is there is there, and the person's comfort lies in the conviction that the surgeon possesses the wherewithal to restore order to any area that is in disarray.

Therefore, how can God heal what we deny? How can God touch what we cover up? How can God grant us pardon, when we won't admit guilt? If my sin is going to come out, then I want it to come out on the Lord's terms and not the enemy's terms. In Hebrews 10:31, it says, "It is a terrifying thing to fall into the hands of the living God." But it's not a terrifying thing to willingly place yourself into the hands of a compassionate God. When you voluntarily place yourself in His hands, then "mercy will triumph over judgment" (James 2:13). Our choice is to either bring our sin to God, where our sin gets judged or to have our sin bring us to God, where we are judged.

A DROPPED PASS AND A SPLINTER

Let me illustrate this by telling you a story where my son Jason is concerned. My office is in my home and is decorated in Pittsburgh Steelers paraphernalia. One of the rules in our house is that no one is allowed in my office while I am away on a trip. While on one of my trips, Jason, who was about eight years old at the time, had a friend over to my house. He took him into my office to show him all my Steelers stuff. Jason showed him the football I have which was signed by all the players from one of their championship teams. Being boys, they soon began throwing the football to each other. Then one of them missed the ball, it hit a wall, causing a clock to hit floor and breaking all the glass that enclosed it.

A few days later, I arrived home and as I came in the door, my son was waiting on me and with tears in his eyes, told me what had happened. Because he voluntarily brought his sin to me, mercy triumphed over judgment. I didn't have to chastise him because his heart was already at the place where any punishment would try and bring him. However, it would have been a different story if when I came home, I had found the damage, then asked who was responsible only to hear everyone say, "Not me." When I would have found it was Jason, he would have found out that it is a terrifying thing to fall into the hands of an angry father. It's my prayer that God will produce in you a desire and hunger for God to judge you right now. That you won't wait until you get to heaven to be judged.

First Timothy 5:24 states that "the sins of some men are quite evident, going before them to judgment; for others, their [sins] follow after." I want to send all my sins on before me and don't want any following after me. To open my sin now will cause me some temporary loss, only to be replaced by some eternal gain. Or I can keep my sin hidden, find some temporary gain, only to be replaced by some eternal loss. The writer of Hebrews wrote, "Let us therefore draw near with confidence to the throne of grace, that we may receive mercy and may find grace to help in time of need" (Hebrews 4:16).

When you draw near to His throne, you will automatically receive mercy. Mercy simply stated is not getting what you deserve. Grace simply stated is getting what you don't deserve. You don't have to do anything to get mercy, except draw near. If you understand this, then when you sin, you won't run from God, but you will run to Him. Mercy is received, but grace has to be found. Mercy will help you with the guilt, but only grace can help you with the sin. Mercy will put the fire out, but only grace can make sure the fire never starts again. Mercy brings forgiveness, but only grace causes cleansing. Mercy restrains God's anger toward your sin, but only grace releases God's love for the sinner.

As you learned in earlier chapters, after receiving the Lord, I turned myself into the authorities. His mercy enabled me to face my sins, and His grace enabled me to put them behind me. His mercy minimized the damage of my sins, and His grace maximized the goodness of the Savior in my life. God will grant you mercy in His judgment in order to give you an opportunity to find His grace for your time of need. The question is "While I'm in His mercy, where can His grace be found?"

When my Jason was six years old, we moved to a new house that was on an acre and half of land with woods all around. One day after hiking in the woods, he came into my office crying because he had somehow gotten a huge splinter in his hand. Since his mom wasn't home, I had to doctor him. With him following me, I went to the medicine cabinet and pulled out a box of band-aids. You could tell by the expression on his face that Jason liked this move. I then took out some Neosporin, which also made him happy. But when I pulled out a needle from his mother's sewing basket, he started to cry and protest, saying, "No, Daddy, no needle, just a band-aid and medicine."

Now, I could have done what he wanted me to do,

and for a while it would have brought some relief. However, sooner or later the medicine would have worn off and then infection would have set in, and his latter condition would have been worse than his former one. He wanted healing without the treatment but the grace for his healing was found in the needle. Like my son, a lot of us want healing without the treatment, but we can't afford to let our wounds be healed superficially. Once we have drawn near to the throne of His grace, He will grant us mercy and give us an opportunity to find the grace we need. My grace was found in a thirty-year prison sentence and also an angry inmate who wanted to hurt me. You need to find where your grace is. Maybe it's in your confession, or in making restitution for something, or in reconciling a broken relationship, or in the renouncing of something you said or did, or in being obedient to something the Lord has told you to do, or by enduring trials, tribulations, and persecutions.

Like Jason's needle, there is an edge to God's judgment, but you can't afford to renounce the treasure because you don't like the darkness. Remember, rightly understood, God's judgments are to be more desired than gold, they are sweeter than honey. They will bring instruction and enlightenment, and will guide us to hidden treasure. They will bring the valleys up and the mountains down, which will cause us to walk on level and smooth paths. Understanding this will cause us to follow after judgments, knowing that God uses the judgment over our lives to produce His righteousness in our lives.

TEN

GET A BIGGER FRYING PAN

God's way leads us through something earthly in order to help us hear something heavenly

I'm called to be a preacher and teacher of God's word. The more I preach, the more absurd I believe preaching is. This is so because through preaching I have the impossible task of trying to get you to see what the Bible says is invisible, to hear what the Bible says is inaudible, and to know something the Bible says surpasses knowledge. For the preaching and teaching to be effective, I need the Holy Spirit to enter into the temporal nature of the words I speak or write and reveal them in such a way that you hear, see, and know something eternal. I refer to this process as "getting a bigger frying pan."

To illustrate my point, allow me to tell you a story about a fisherman who was on a bridge fishing in a channel that led out to the Gulf of Mexico where several others were fishing as well. While they were all there, one of the fisherman began to do something strange with the fish he was catching. After he caught a fish, he would hold it up and, depending on it size, would either throw it back or put it in his bucket. Now, that wouldn't be strange if he was throwing back all the smaller fish and keeping the bigger ones, but he was doing the opposite. He was throwing back all the big fish and only keeping the smaller ones. When asked about this behavior, he said, "My frying pan is just so big, so if they don't fit into my frying pan, I throw them back." I guess he never thought of getting a bigger frying pan—and maybe you haven't either.

The challenge we all face when we read the Bible or listen to sermons is not to discard what God is wanting to say to us because it doesn't fit into our frying pan—our nice, narrow, comfortable, easy-to-understand theological thinking. Instead, we need to allow God to give us a bigger frying pan by allowing the Holy Spirit to enlarge our capacity to know Him, because there are things God wants to say to us that are bigger than our present capacity to understand.

One of the books I read early in my Christian experience was by J. B. Phillips and was titled *Your God Is Too Small*. After I read his book, I realized my conception of God was small, childish, and limited. I allowed my own personal comfort to determine how big I allowed God to become in my thinking. My fear was that the bigger and more powerful He was, the more He would expect from me. My limit on God was a feeble attempt on my part to control what God could or would do in my life. I did this to my own detriment because there were many times when I needed a bigger and more powerful God, but the same box I had placed Him in to control what He did in me also kept Him from conquering certain things for me. From that point on, I determined I was going to seek after the bigness of God by allowing Him to enlarge my capacity to know Him, or as I have already stated, to "give me a bigger frying pan."

Consider for a moment how incredibly big and awesome our God is. In order to get you to see how big your Creator is, let's get a glimpse of how big His creation is. To accomplish this, let's take a quick trip out into the universe at the speed of light, which is 186,000 miles a second, or 11,000,000 miles a minute, or 660,000,000 miles an hour, or 15, 840,000,000 miles a day. A light year is how far you would travel in a year at the speed of light which is 5,781,600,000,000 miles. At that speed you would blow by the Moon in 1.3 seconds, reach the sun in 8 minutes, and would leave our solar system in five hours.

After you leave our solar system, it would take four light years to reach the nearest star to our solar system. Going through our galaxy, the Milky Way, you would pass a star every five light years. Once you get out of the Milky Way, then space really opens up. The next galaxy, Andronomy, is two million light years away. Galaxies come in groups. Some have as few as three galaxies, our own galaxy is one of a cluster of 17 galaxies, which astronomers call, in all serious-ness, the local group. The largest group of galaxies, Hercules, would take us 300 million lights years to reach. It contains 10,000 galaxies, each containing billions of stars. In all, there are at least ten billion galaxies in the known universe. Now think about all that in the context of what Paul wrote in Colossians 1:20-22:

> From beginning to end He's there, towering far above everything. So spacious is He, so roomy, that everything that comes from God finds its proper place in Him without crowding. Not only that, but all the broken and dislocated pieces of the universe, people and circumstances, get properly fixed and fit together in vibrant harmonies, all of because of His death and His blood that poured down from the Cross (MSG).

If our God is bigger than the universe, then He is big enough to take care of us and make all the changes necessary in our lives.

Ephesians 1:16-17 is the beginning of a prayer Paul prayed for the Ephesians: "I do not cease giving thanks for you, while making mention of you in my prayers; that the God of our Lord Jesus Christ, the Father of glory, may give to you a spirit of wisdom and of revelation in the knowledge of Him." This passage says that in order to know Jesus, you must be given a spirit of revelation. Have you ever had it happen to you where you were having your daily devotional time, read a passage from the Scriptures you have read many times, only this time see it like you were reading it for the first time? This occurs because this time while reading it, the Spirit of God opened your finite mind to understand the infinite wonders of this particular word.

Not only were you gaining His knowledge, but this knowledge was imparting His life. This experience not only caused you to know more, it also released power for you to become more, and a passion for you to do more. Then in the excitement of this experience, you usually do something stupid. You go and share your revelation with another person. I call this stupid because most of the time when you share this revelation with someone, they throw cold water on your experience by responding with a "I already know that." You know they neither know it the way you know it nor see it the way you saw it, because if they did, they would be as excited at you are. The problem is that you can't impart by articulation what you received by revelation.

You may be able to impart the knowledge of the revelation you received, but only the Spirit of God can impart the power to be and the passion to do that all His revelation represents. Revelation comes when our capacity to know God is enlarged. Simply speaking, revelation is God helping you know something that you couldn't know unless He helped you. The problem that we have as we seek to understand the Bible is although it was penned by men, it was written by God and therefore contains infinite knowledge. The struggle often comes when we try to evaluate His infinite knowledge with our finite mind. Revelation occurs when God enlarges our finite mind in order to receive His infinite knowledge.

To illustrate this, I want to tell you another story about my son Jason. When he was three years old, we lived in Orlando, Florida. In the summertime, it would rain every day at about 3:30 p.m. One day he and I were in the car together and after it rained, he asked me, "Daddy where does rain come from?" One of the few subjects I was good in at school was science. Therefore, I had vast knowledge about rain. My dilemma was to take my vast knowledge, reduce it, simplify it, and then inject it into this three-year-old's capacity to understand. I was able to reduce my knowledge to one sentence but even as simple as that sentence was, it was still too big for his "frying pan" or his capacity to understand. Instead of helping to understand rain, it just confused him further, because his response was, "Okay, but why?" This is our exact dilemma when the Holy Spirit tries to take the infinite knowledge of God, reduce it, simplify it and then inject it into our capacity to understand spiritual things.

In John 16:12, we see that Jesus had this same problem with His disciples when He said, "I have many more things to say to you, but you cannot bear them now." In other words, their frying pan was too small. Jesus understood the disciples' capacity to understand spiritual things hadn't matured sufficiently for Him to say certain things to them. The *Contemporary English Version* renders verse 12, "I have much more to say to you, but right now it would be more than you could understand" and *The Message* says it this way: "I still have many things to tell you, but you can't handle them now."

Verse 13 goes on to tell us that it's the Holy Spirit's job to enlarge (give us a bigger frying pan) our capacity to grasp more of Him, "but when He, the Spirit of truth, comes, He will guide you into all the truth." The implication is that the Holy Spirit will lead us through some earthly experience that will tax, stretch, and enlarge us so we can hear something heavenly. Most Christians get a revelation in the midst or at the end of a trial or tribulation. Another example of this is found in Exodus 3:7-8 where God appeared to Moses in a burning bush and said,

> "I have surely seen the affliction of My people who are in Egypt, and have given heed to their cry because of their taskmasters, for I am aware of their sufferings. So I have come down to deliver them from the power of the Egyptians, and to

bring them up from that land to a good and spa-
cious land, to a land flowing with milk and honey."

God only tells the Israelites the part they can bear and
grasp so they can move forward in faith. God waited until
they left Egypt and arrived at the border of the Promised
Land to show them all that was going to be involved in their
Exodus experience.

In Numbers 13, Moses sent out twelve men to spy
out this land God has promised to give them, and they come
back with this report. Verses 27-28 state, "We explored the
land and it does flow with milk and honey; and here is some
of its fruit. But the people who live there are powerful, and
their cities are very large and well-fortified. Even worse,
we saw the descendants of the giants there." God didn't do
this to trick them. He knew after being slaves for 400 years
where they struggled each day just to save their lives, they
could not have handled the thought of being soldiers where
they would be required to risk their lives.

In fact, in Exodus 13:17-18 we are told, "When
Pharaoh finally let the people go, God did not lead them on
the road that runs through Philistine territory, even though
that was the shortest way from Egypt to the Promised Land.
God said, "If the people are faced with a battle, they might
change their minds and return to Egypt" (NLT). God knew
if they had actually faced battle at this time in their deliverance, they would have changed their mind and returned
to Egypt, preferring bondage over battle. They would rather
have wasted their lives by preserving self than sowing their
lives in service to the Savior.

God waited until they witnessed His power through
the plagues before He brought them out of Egypt and parted
of the Red Sea. He waited until they experienced His provision as seen in making the bitter water sweet, providing man-
na in the morning and quail at night, and the water from the
rock, before He told them about His purpose for their lives.
In Egypt, they were a nation of slaves, but in the Promised
Land, they were going to be a nation of kings. In Egypt, they
were a people used to being ruled, but in the Promised Land

they would be a people who were going to reign. In Egypt, God sovereignly delivered them by channeling His power through the staff of Moses. In the Promised Land, He was going to channel His power through their lives.

The time in the wilderness was designed to teach each of them how to walk in the power that delivered them. God was hoping the demonstration of His power for them would cause an imitation of that power by them. Two of the twelve spies, Joshua and Caleb, had their frying pans sufficiently enlarged to where they said, "We should by all means go up and take possession of it, for we shall surely overcome it" (Numbers 13:30-31) but the other ten said, "We are not able to go up against the people, for they are too strong for us." The difference between the two and the ten is that the two allowed God to guide them through the truth that the same God who had *saved* them with power was then *sending* them with power.

We find an example of this in the New Testament when Jesus was trying to tell His disciples that he was the Savior of the whole world, as stated in John 3:16: "For God so loved the world, that He gave His only begotten Son, that whoever believes in Him should not perish, but have eternal life" and in John 10:16, "And I have other sheep, which are not of this fold; I must bring them also, and they shall hear My voice; and they shall become one flock with one shepherd." What their frying pan allowed them to hear was, "God so loved the Jewish world" or "the other sheep that He had were other Jewish communities in the world."

In Acts 1:8, He told his disciples, "You will receive power when the Holy Spirit has come upon you; and you shall be My witnesses both in Jerusalem, and in all Judea and Samaria, and even to the remotest part of the earth." What they heard was, "We will receive power to be His witnesses to the Jews in Jerusalem, and to the Jews Judea, Samaria, and to the Jews in the remotest part of the earth." I know that is what they heard because that is what they practiced. They would not allow the gospel of Jesus Christ to break out of the Jewish culture.

Consequently, the Holy Spirit had to take Peter, one

of the disciples, and guide him into some new truth. First, however, He had to enlarge him before He spoke to him. This process is described in Acts 10. Early in this chapter, Peter was at Simon the Tanner's house. Peter was on the roof of the house praying when he had a vision. In the vision, a large sheet was let down and in it were all kinds of animals that were unclean for a Jewish person to eat. In the midst of this vision, Peter heard the voice of the Lord say, "Arise, kill and eat." Peter assumed this a test from God to see if he would stay true to the teachings of the Law. The reason I know that was what Peter was thinking is because he was about to say "No, God," and we only want to say no if that is what we think He wants to hear. Much to Peter's surprise after he said no to God, he heard God respond by saying, "Do not call anything impure that I have made clean. This happened three times, and immediately the sheet was taken back to heaven."

While he is trying to make sense of the vision and God's responses, three Gentiles showed up at Simon's house looking for Peter with a crazy story about a Roman centurion who had an angelic visitation during which he was told to send for Peter. The proof that their story was true is the fact that those Gentiles knew where Peter was staying. Normally Peter wouldn't go anywhere with Gentiles because contact with them could have rendered him unclean and unholy. However, he had seen this vision three times and there were three Gentiles at his door. In the midst of his deliberations, the Spirit told Peter not to hesitate to go with them. Can you see how this experience the Holy Spirit was leading Peter through was stretching and enlarging him, which resulted in him getting a bigger frying pan?

Still not sure of why he was being sent to a Roman centurion's home, Peter was then invited to preach the gospel to all who had gathered. When he saw the hunger and thirst these Gentiles had to know about Jesus, he got what I refer to as a "now word." His frying pan had gotten bigger and his knowledge of God was about to get bigger as well. Acts 10:34 states, "Now I understand, God is no respecter of persons." Peter was essentially saying, "Now I get it, God is not partial. The gospel of Jesus is for everyone, everywhere." Jesus was probably in heaven at that moment saying, "Finally, one of my disciples has been enlarged enough to bear this word that I am Savior of the whole world." As a result of Peter's revelation, the gospel was freed from its Jewish bonds and was preached to the whole world. Revelation or a now word brings us truth and truth brings freedom, not only to us, but through us to the whole world.

A PERSONAL EXAMPLE

Let me give you some personal examples of getting a bigger frying pan which resulted in a "now word" for my life. Prior to becoming a Christian, I hitchhiked a lot. When I hitchhiked, I loved it when Christians would pick me up because I learned that if I looked interested in their spiel about Christ, they would go out of their way to take me further than where they were going. I also learned that if I cried and acted like I accepted Christ, they would either buy me a meal or give me some money to help me on my way. My point is that before I was a Christian I heard about Christ, how on a cross He died for my sins, and that through faith in Him I could have not only eternal life, but also an abundant, changed and meaningful life. However, in my pursuit of a life full of pleasure and power that I thought would lead me to real life, I couldn't hear those words.

That pursuit of pleasure and power didn't lead me to real life but caused me to take the life of a real person. It was this experience that emptied me of everything I thought I wanted for my life so that I could get in on everything that He wanted in and through my life. I wasn't able to hear the words of His hope until I came to a place of utter hopelessness. I wasn't able to be filled with what He has until I was emptied of what I had.

That night, as I sat thinking my life was over and contemplating suicide, I heard the words of the Savior telling me that the end of me was the beginning with Him. Like Peter at the centurion's house, I said to myself, "Now I understand what those people who picked me up while I was hitchhiking were trying to tell me." The girl who shared Christ with me only used a few words in the context of a few Scriptures, but I heard more than what she was saying.

I not only heard that I was going to heaven, but I also heard that no matter what was going to happen while I was still on earth, everything was going to be alright. I not only heard that my sins were forgiven but I also heard that I was given His righteousness. Though the Lord did not cause the circumstances that led me to take someone's life, His Spirit was with me, leading me and causing all that happened to work together for my good. Before my heart could be enlarged, my life had to be reduced. As a result, at the lowest point of my earthly life, I was able to hear the highest call of His heavenly voice.

Another example of God's Spirit leading me through something earthly so I could hear something heavenly has to do with an experience I had in prison. As I mentioned in the last chapter, the prison I was sent to was one of the most violent in the state of Florida. Sexual assaults happened frequently. Being young and fairly good looking, I was told by other inmates in the county jail that once I got to prison I was going have a hard time. I was told by one person that I would probably get raped within the first couple of days of being in prison. Needless to say, I was scared.

Once I got to prison, a lot of those fears were realized in that a lot of inmates looked upon me as an object of their lust. They would whistle at me and make crude remarks. Each night I went to bed with the fear that I was going to be raped. This fear caused me to lose sleep, and if I did sleep, I didn't sleep soundly. Though I had to deal with the threat of rape on a daily basis, God was with me and protected me and after a year had gone by, no one had acted on their threats.

Though God had delivered me from the actual act of rape, I still dealt with daily fear of rape, thinking that the coming night was the night when someone would act on their threats. By this time my lack of sound sleep was beginning to take its toll on me mentally, emotionally, and physically. I desperately prayed that God would remove this fear that was dominating my life. Each morning I would pray that God would deliver me from fear, but each night the fear would return. I was perplexed as to why God wouldn't answer this prayer, so I reminded Him of his promise in Matthew 7:7, that if "I asked then I would receive." But with all my asking, I was not receiving.

While this was happening, I received a package in the mail from a Christian woman who was writing me. I had asked her if she would send me some toiletries and a pair of basketball shoes. I love to play basketball, but for the previous year I had to play in the work boots the prison had issued me. Also, in prison shoes mean a lot to inmates. Since all the clothing is the same, the only way we had to make a fashion statement was by the shoes that we wore. With that in mind I had ordered a particular type of basketball shoe.

I asked this woman if she would send me a pair of Converse All Stars with blue suede, red stars, and plaid shoe-laces. When someone receives a package, all the other inmates come around to see what he received. When I pulled out these shoes, everybody nodded with approval. As I was lacing the shoes anticipating wearing them that night out on the court, I heard the still small voice of the Lord say to me. "Son, I want you to give these shoes to Raymond Brinson."

My first reaction was that this had to be the devil, because God wouldn't ask me to give away something I wanted so badly for a long time. Yet every time I went to go put the shoes on, I sensed that God wanted me to give them to Raymond. To make things even more difficult, I didn't like Raymond. He was a new inmate, having gotten saved in the county jail, and he was on fire for the Lord. Until he had arrived, most of the other Christian brothers looked to me for leadership, but Raymond was far more knowledgeable, more joyful, and more courageous than I, so therefore the other inmates gravitated to him. So not only did he receive the following I had, he was now going to get my shoes. I had received the shoes on Wednesday and on the following Saturday I decided to obey the Lord and take the shoes to Raymond. When I gave them to him, he thanked me and told me that He had been praying for a pair of shoes, and wouldn't you guess it, he wore the same size as I did.

Though I lost a pair of shoes that day, I received two

things in their place. That night I slept like a baby. For the first time in a year, I slept without fear. It was at this time that I began to understand that "ask and you shall receive" is only one half of a truth, and the other half is "give and it shall be given unto you" (Luke 6:38). It was when I freely gave my shoes to Raymond that I freely received my deliverance from fear. The moment I asked God for deliverance from fear, He was both willing and able to give it to me, but He wouldn't give to me what I wanted until I gave something He wanted. As a result of this experience, I continue to ask God for things that I want, but once I do, I then look for the opportunity to give what He wants.

The second thing I gained that day was a lifelong friend. Raymond and I were able to do many exploits for the Kingdom of God while we were in prison. He got out of a prison a year after I did, so I went and picked him up and had him live with me until he got situated. Raymond was also a part of my wedding, and he was the person with whom I started a church in 1986. Raymond has gone on to be with the Lord in January 2019. I will miss him dearly.

As the Spirit guided me through this experience, I was led to the truth of Acts 20:35 which says that "it is more blessed to give than to receive." This verse simply means that more happens spiritually when you give something then when you receive something. If I would have kept those shoes, the only value they would have brought me would be some temporary approval of other inmates and temporary comfort in playing basketball. Within weeks they would have lost their beauty and within a couple of months, they would have worn out. When I gave them away, however, I received an everlasting trust in God's ability to take care of me and a friendship that will last through the ages.

Let me close this chapter by encouraging you to pray and ask God to give you a "bigger frying pan." Once you do, you had better fasten your seat belt, for the Holy Spirt will begin to take you for a ride that will lead you into new truth.

ELEVEN

THE BREEZE IS
WORTH THE FLIES

*God's way of using how we
receive His minister to determine
how much of His ministry is
released*

In January of 1984 as I was preparing to launch a para-church organization, I was in my study praying when I had what I can only call a vision. In it, I saw a group of families loading covered wagons with all their worldly possessions. These families were preparing to make a journey from one part of the country to another. The handwritten words painted on the sides of their wagons, "California or Bust," indicated they knew that their journey would be long and dangerous, but their facial expressions were ones of joy and expectation.

As I watched this scene unfold, I heard the words they were speaking to one another and realized the journey was the source of both their joy and also expectation. For this reason, they were willing to leave the safety of the known to pursue the possibility of the unknown. The words they were speaking to one another again and again were "there's gold in them there hills."

Then the scene shifted, and I found myself in the rafters of a church looking down on a congregation during a worship service. What caught my attention was the angelic activity that was going on in the atmosphere around this congregation. I saw angels descending and ascending back and forth from heaven. The atmosphere was charged with excitement and joy. As I watched, I heard the angels repeatedly say something to each other. Upon hearing it, I realized the source of their excitement and joy. What they were saying was simply "there's gold in them there lives."

Right after this vision ended, I heard the Lord say to me through a still small voice, "The last great outpouring of the Spirit was *on* the church but the next great outpouring is going to be *out from* the church." He is now going to release from the Church the gold He instilled in the Church, which brought great value to our lives, in order to bring great value to the world. In Ephesians 1:18, Paul gave evidence to this when he prayed "that the eyes of our hearts may be enlightened, so that we may know . . . what are the riches of the glory of His inheritance in the saints." God has placed the riches of His inheritance in us. This inheritance is not just for us but for others as well. The implication of this is that no one of us has all the inheritance, but each one of us in the Body has a portion of the inheritance.

God does this so we will mutually be dependent upon one another. This means in order for me to get all my inheritance, I have to accept all those He has joined me to, has sent to me, and has sent me to. I have found that God seldom answers prayers directly, He usually finds those who have that portion of His inheritance I need and then sends those people to me. As Christians, we are God's economy, so when God wants to do something in the world, He spends His people to do or give it. Furthermore, God gets this people from His savings account which is comprised of those people He has saved. Therefore, if you are saved, then God can and will spend you on behalf of others. In light of this, the question that needs to be answered is: How do I release the gold or the inheritance that others are carrying for me and transfer it from their lives into mine?

Psalm 118:25-26 gives us some insight and instruction on how we can accomplish this, "Save us, we pray, O Lord! O Lord, we pray, send us prosperity! Blessed is he who comes in the name of the Lord! We bless you from the house of the Lord" (ESV). In this passage, a group of God's people were praying and asking God for two things. The first was salvation. The Hebrew word for salvation is *yasha,* which means *wholeness, deliverance, and victory.* These people did not just want eternal salvation, but *total* salvation. They wanted the broken areas of their lives to become whole, they wanted to be set free from the areas where they were bound, and they wanted victory in the areas in which had been defeated.

The second thing they asked for was prosperity. The Hebrew word for *prosperity* is *tsalach* which means *to advance, make progress, succeed, or to be profitable.* These people were not just praying to get better, they were praying to do better. Not only are they praying for their brokenness, they were also praying for their usefulness. Salvation has to do with restoring the person, and prosperity has to do restoring God's purpose for that person. It's the idea that God not only saves us from something but also for something.

Unlike some Christians, however, these people knew what to do next. After praying, they began to look for the one God was going to send to them with the answers to their prayers. The *Living Bible* renders the passage in Psalm 118 this way: "O Lord, please help us. Save us. Give us success. Blessed is the one who is coming, the one sent by the Lord." They understood that God would answer their prayer by filling and equipping, and then sending someone into their life.

Not only did they know to look for the answers from the ones who God sent, but they also knew how to receive and treat them when they arrived. They knew in order to get the blessing from God, they first had to be a blessing for God. The Hebrew word for *blessed* used in verse 26 is *barak,* which means *to endue with power for prosperity.* They knew they had to prosper the one who was sent in order to release the prosperity they carried for the ones who prayed.

They knew if they blessed the messenger into their lives, it would then release the message for their lives. They understood the principle of receiving and releasing. The way you receive the person God sends to you determines how much of what they carry for you is released to you. The New Testament equivalent of this principle is found in Matthew 23:37-39 which states,

> "O Jerusalem, Jerusalem, who kills the prophets and stones those who are sent to her! How often I wanted to gather your children together, the way a hen gathers her chicks under her wings, and you were unwilling. Behold, your house is being left to you desolate! For I say to you, from now on you shall not see Me until you say, 'Blessed is He who comes in the name of the Lord!'" (NASB).

In this passage there are three phrases I want to examine more closely in order to get a better understanding of what Jesus was trying to communicate.

THREE PHRASES

The first phrase is "who are sent." The Greek word for sent is *apostello,* which means *to order one to go to an appointed place or person*. In verse 37, Jesus was grieving over the fact that the Father had sent prophets to Jerusalem who were empowered and equipped to unite, protect and care for them, but because they didn't recognize them as coming from God, they stoned and killed them instead of receiving them.

The second phrase is "your house is left desolate." The Greek word for desolate is *eremos,* which means *to be deprived of the aid and protection which is needed for prosperity and to lay waste as a result of neglect*—like a flock deserted by a shepherd. In this situation, however, it's not the shepherd who deserts the flock but the flock that deserts the shepherd, all because they didn't see the one who was sent as being the shepherd. Jerusalem was being left desolate because it had deprived

itself of the aid and protection it needed in order to prosper
when it would not receive the ones being sent to it.

The third and final phrase is "from now on you shall
not see Me until you say, 'Blessed is He who comes in the
name of the Lord!'" The Greek word for *blessed* is *eulogeo,*
which means *to cause to prosper, to make happy, to bestow blessings on.* It's not just saying "be blessed" but doing those things
that will ensure the one God has sent to me is blessed. There
Jesus was stating that His people would not see Him, perceive His presence, or partake of His provision and power
His presence carried until they learned how to bless the one
who carried the blessing for their lives.

We further see this principle of "receiving and releasing" in Matthew 10:40 which states, "He who receives you
receives Me, and he who receives Me receives Him who
sent Me." Jesus was telling His disciples that the Father had
sent Him to them and was equipped by the Father for them.
He in turn was sending them to others with the promise
that they would carry for others what He had carried for
them. The one who is being sent carries the authority and
the power of the one who sends him. Jesus confirmed this
when He said in John 20:21, "As the Father has sent Me, I
also send you."

Years ago, I heard a story about a four-year-old boy
who had gone to bed, but as soon as he fell asleep a thun-
derstorm came through the area and the loud thunder awakened and scared this little boy. He was so scared that he ran
down the hall into his parents' bedroom and jumped into
their bed. The father, who was a Christian, took his son back
to his own bed and assured him that there nothing to be
afraid of because Jesus was right in the room with him and
He wouldn't allow anything to hurt him.

This seemed to comfort the little boy until the next
loud clap of thunder which caused him to once again get
out of his bed and jump into bed with his parents. The father once more took him back to his own bed, assuring
him again that Jesus was in the room with him. When there
was another burst of thunder, the father found his son in
bed with them once again. This time before his father could

carry him back to his own bed, the little boy said to his dad, "I know Jesus is in my room with me, but I need someone with skin on."

The application for our lives should be clear. When the Lord sends us to someone, we become God with skin on for that person. Jesus the ministry is placed in us the ministers for the purpose of releasing the ministry of Christ into the lives of others. Whether or not this ministry is released will be determined by how those who need the ministry receive the minister. The Greek word for *"receive"* in verse 40 is *dechomai,* which means *to receive favorably, to receive with hospitality, or to treat the one who was sent with generous kindness.* Jesus was saying if you receive with hospitality the one who He sends, we will see and get Him, and if we get Him, we get all the power and provision of the One who sent Him.

In Luke 10:16, Jesus told His disciples the opposite of what He told them in Matthew 10:40: "The one who rejects you rejects Me; and he who rejects Me rejects the One who sent Me." The Greek word for reject is *atheteo* which mean *to void, nullify or neutralize the power that produces the effects.* In other words, when we reject the one God sends to us, we also neutralize the power and the provision they carry for us. I can't tell you how many times I missed out on God's provision and power because I didn't believe the one He sent could possibly be from God. Thus, instead of receiving them, I judged and criticized them, thereby neutralizing all that they had for me.

For example, there have been many times that I came to a church service when we would have a guest speaker and I would find myself judging the speaker instead of listening to him. It may be because he was dressed too casually, or had a particular accent, or was overweight, or repeated a particular phrase too often. Whatever the reason, I didn't receive him but was in fact rejecting him. My criticism caused me to take the posture that he didn't have much to offer me, not realizing it was my criticism that was neutralizing what he did have for me.

It would surprise me when others in the same service seemed to be blessed by what the speaker was saying. They would take copious notes and say amen after almost every sentence. In the midst of this, I would think to myself, *Why are these people getting so excited about this fluff?* The truth is that it was only fluff to me but not to them. Because they received the minister, they released the ministry into their lives. The words they heard were anointed by the Holy Spirit. They were hearing the word within the Word and as a result, they got in on the provision and power this man carried for them.

Let's go back and look at Matthew 10:41: "He who receives a prophet in the name of a prophet shall receive a prophet's reward; and he who receives a righteous man in the name of a righteous man shall receive a righteous man's reward." This verse tells us that in order to get what a prophet has, we must embrace and hospitably receive the prophet. What the prophet carries for our lives is defined as a reward in this verse. The Greek word for *reward* there is *misthos,* which means *dues paid for work* or *labor which is rewarded in some way*. It means the prophet who has labored by seeking God on our behalf has some provision or empowerment for our lives.

The implication is that it cost the prophet something to have what he or she has for us. But now, we must labor to get the reward of their labor. It's not laboring to produce the reward, but it is laboring to receive the reward. It takes work and will cost us to receive someone with an open and kind spirit. It has the idea that as you enter into the reward of their labor, they should be able to enter into the reward of our labor. Galatians 6:6 substantiates this idea when it says, "And let the one who is taught the word share all good things with him who teaches."

For example, it is in keeping with this verse to take it a little further and say, "He who receives a worship leader will get a worship leader's reward." What do you think would happen if each Sunday before the service started, you would go to the worship team and seek to bless them in some way, knowing they have labored through prayer and practice to bring you the reward of vibrant, life-changing worship? Do you think your giving to them will make a difference in how much you receive from them?

Jesus said in Luke 6:38, "Give, and it will be given to you; good measure, pressed down, shaken together, running over, they will pour into your lap. For by your standard of measure it will be measured to you in return." Notice that the "good measure, pressed down, shaken together, running over" doesn't happen until you give something. We could continue this thread by saying, "He who receives a pastor will get a pastor's reward," or "He who receives a teacher will get a teacher's reward."

This principle of "receiving and releasing" even works in the natural. When I lived in Pennsylvania, we had a power transformer go out where we lived causing a power failure for us. The power company determined the problem was caused by all the trees that had grown up around the transformer. To correct this problem, they sent out a crew to cut down the trees. I had a problem with the men who were sent, for they all had long hair, smoked, and used foul language. As a result, I didn't receive them with hospitality. Instead, I kept my distance and made sure my children kept their distance as well. After a day of watching these men work hard, I realized my attitude toward them was wrong. Therefore, the next day my family and I brought them water and soft drinks throughout the day. In talking with them I discovered they had great personalities and were gentle and respectful to my children. In fact, while we were with them, they didn't smoke or cuss around us.

When they were done, they took some extra time to cut the trees into firewood for our wood burning stove and they gave us all the rest of the wood in the form of mulch for our garden. By receiving them with hospitality, I received about a $1,000.00 worth of firewood and mulch. Because I received a tree cutter, I released a tree cutter's reward.

If everything I have written so far is true, then here is the "big question." What if the person who is sent to us is foolish, weak, or flawed? Here is the "big answer." Those are the only kind of people God has to use. In 2 Corinthians 4:7, Paul told us the ministry we carry is a "treasure" and referred to the people God uses to carry this treasure as perishable and weak containers: "But this precious treasure—this light and power that now shine within us—is held in perishable containers, that is, in our weak bodies. So everyone can see that our glorious power is from God and is not our own" (NLT). Another translation refers to the carriers of the treasure as "earthen vessels," earthen indicating something weak, flawed, or imperfect. What God does is the treasure, whom He sends is the earthen vessel. We need to make sure we don't let the earthiness of the vessels God sends keep us from the treasures they carry.

AN EARTHEN VESSEL

When I first entered the ministry, I almost deprived myself of a treasure God had for me because I didn't like the earthiness of the vessel He was using to bring me the treasure. In September of 1983, my wife and I moved to Orlando, Florida to work in a para-church organization. Once there, we started attending a church near where we lived. It was a great church, with a great pastor and excellent preaching and worship. As soon as we got there, we started hearing about a particular revival meeting they held every year. We were told that an evangelist from West Palm Beach came each January and held nightly meetings that could last for weeks, depending on how powerfully the Spirit was moving. As January got closer and closer, everybody in the church, including Diane and I, were getting more and more excited.

Finally, the first night of meetings arrived, the church was packed, and the atmosphere was charged with eager expectation. Diane and I were on the front row eagerly anticipating all God was going to do through these meetings. However, when the evangelist came on the platform, I was shocked and offended by what I saw. This evangelist represented everything I didn't like in preachers. He was dressed in a three-piece ivory white suit. He had on a pair of red patent leather shoes, a red sash tied around his waist, and a red carnation pinned to his suit coat. He didn't wear a tie and his shirt was open down to the middle of his chest, making it easy to see the many gold chains and crosses he wore around his neck. He had a ring on almost every finger, a gold watch on one arm, and a gold bracelet on the other.

He was about 60 years old with a thick head of hair that was white and long. When he spoke he would scream, throw the microphone in the air, and walk over pews. If I wasn't sitting on the front row, I would have stormed out in righteous indignation. As I sat there listening to him, I began to realize that God's Spirit was beginning to move in the service. Though I didn't like the way he was dressed or the style he used when preaching, I couldn't deny the fact that what he preached had power. When he was done, he started praying for people and I saw many get converted, healed, and delivered. He even came and prayed for me, and his prayers touched and healed me in a way that changed my life from that point on.

After the meeting, we went home, but I stayed up after Diane went to bed and, with my Bible in my lap, I prayed, asking God how He could use such a flamboyant showboat of a person like I had seen. As I was praying, I sensed God speak to my heart these words: "Son, just because you don't like a flamboyant, showboat kind of person, doesn't mean that others don't." He went on to show me that it is the flamboyance and showboating that opens certain people's heart to the message of the gospel. It is for this reason that He has and uses these kinds of earthen vessels.

When I got done praying, I happened to look down and saw my Bible was open to the Romans 14:4 which says, "Who are you to judge the servant of another? To his own master he stands or falls; and stand he will, for the Lord is able to make him stand" (NASB). The *New Living Translation* says, "Who are you to condemn God's servants? They are responsible to the Lord, so let him tell them whether they are right or wrong. The Lord's power will help them do as they should." While I was sitting in that meeting condemning the servant of God because of the earthiness of his vessel, God was in that meeting helping him with His power to do the things he was called and equipped by God to do. I am grateful that in spite of myself, God allowed me to get in on the treasure this man carried for my life.

This experience taught me that God will use someone's imperfections to reveal and carry out His perfect will for our lives. I don't know why I was so surprised that God could use a man like this evangelist, for He has and continues to use me. I'm sure there have been a lot of people who have missed out on the treasure I carry because they couldn't get past the earthiness of my vessel. A related verse to 2 Corinthians 4:7 is 1 Corinthians 1:26-29, which tells us that God uses our foolishness to bring others His wisdom, uses our weaknesses to bring others His strength, and uses use what is naught in our lives to bring to naught things in the lives of others.

To further illustrate this principle, allow me to tell you a story about my wife's grandmother. She was a widow who lived in Michigan until she was ninety years old (she has since passed away). She was one of the sweetest ladies I had ever met and was also a tremendous cook. With that said, none of her children or grandchildren liked to go and visit her during the summer. Not only did Grandma not have air conditioning in her house, she didn't like flies which caused her to keep all the windows shut. This caused the temperature in her house to remain in the mid-nineties. I once told my children that it was important to live for God, because if they didn't, they might end up in hell and whether they believed it or not, hell was hotter than Grandma's house. Once while on a visit, I tried to convince Grandma to open up one of the windows so we could enjoy the breeze that was blowing outside. She protested by telling me about the flies, which I responded to with this statement, "But grandma the breeze is worth the flies."

My point is that I still have some flies that buzz around my life which can and will irritate others, but I also carry a breeze from the Holy Spirit, and for those who have put up with my flies, they get to enjoy my breeze. I hope they would tell anyone who asked, "The breeze was worth the flies." The evangelist from West Palm Beach definitely had some flies, but he also carried a breeze of the Holy Spirit. I am grateful that I put down my judgmental fly swatter long enough to get in on the breeze, and my testimony is "the breeze was worth the flies."

Even though Jesus was perfect, there were still many

people who didn't get in on the heavenly breeze that He carried because of their perception that He had some flies. Matthew 13:54–58 attests to this:

> He returned to Nazareth, his hometown. When he taught there in the synagogue, everyone was astonished and said, "Where does he get his wisdom and his miracles? He's just a carpenter's son, and we know Mary, his mother, and his brothers— James, Joseph, Simon, and Judas. All his sisters live right here among us. What makes him so great?" And they were deeply offended and refused to believe in him. Then Jesus told them, "A prophet is honored everywhere except in his own hometown and among his own family." And so he did only a few miracles there because of their unbelief (NLT).

The people who knew Jesus the best had a harder time receiving from Him. They perceived flies of being the son of a common carpenter and a member of an ordinary Nazareth family and that kept the majority of them from enjoying the miraculous breeze of the Holy Spirit He carried. Because they couldn't receive Him as the Son of God, then He wasn't able to release the inheritance of the Father He had. But there were a few in Nazareth who didn't focus on the perception of the flies but on the reality of the breeze and they got the miracle Jesus carried for them.

What about you? Are you going to part of the majority who is offended by the flies or are you going to part of the few who opens us the windows of your heart and enjoys the breeze?

TWELVE

DRY TIMES ARE FOR PROMOTION, NOT PUNISHMENT

God's way of taking that which stimulates thirst to produce a pool that satisfies thirst

"God uses broken things." This is a phrase I read in a book I was reading. The first thing that struck me about the phrase is how contrary it is to the way I respond to broken things, which I usually discard. Whereas I find something useful until it is broken, God doesn't find something useful until *after* it is broken. It was not until Jacob's natural strength was broken, when "his hip was wrenched" (Genesis 32:25) at Peniel, that he came to the point where God could clothe him with spiritual power. It wasn't until Gideon's 300 specially chosen soldiers "broke the jars that were in their hands" (Judges 7:19) that the hidden light of the torches shone forth, bringing terror to their enemies. There are many other examples in the Bible of "brokenness producing usefulness" but these are enough to show us it's not until there is a brokenness in one's outer life that there can be no usefulness in one's inner life.

In this chapter, I want to discuss the process that God uses to move His people from brokenness to usefulness. In order to do this, let's look at Isaiah 35:7-8: "And the scorched land will become a pool, and the thirsty ground springs of water; in the haunt of jackals, its resting place, grass becomes reeds and rushes. And a highway will be there, a roadway, and it will be called the Highway of Holiness." I want to look at some phrases in this passage that will help us glean some insights into this important process through which God wants to take all Christians.

The first insight is found in verse seven: "And the scorched land will become a pool, and the thirsty ground springs of water." This seems confusing to most people because it doesn't indicate that while you are in a "scorched land God will give you a pool," but rather "that the scorched land itself will become a pool." The very thing that creates thirst will, if you persevere, become the very thing that quenches your thirst. The very thing that breaks you is also the thing that will make you. If you understand this, then when you are in dry times, you won't seek to be delivered from it but sift through it, knowing there has to be a pool somewhere in the midst of it.

The idea the writer is trying to communicate is that in the midst of something seemingly bad, something good can be found. I have a minister friend who had a dream in which he was in a warehouse and the name of the warehouse was "bad experiences." There was a truck at the loading dock where boxes from the warehouse were being loaded. On the side of the boxes were the words "good things." He believed God was telling him that you can always find "good things in bad experiences." It's what Isaiah 45:3 says, "God will give you treasures hidden in the darkness" or Jeremiah 15:19 where God says that "[I] will help you extract the precious from the worthless."

God uses dry times for two reasons. The first is to get you to thirst afresh for Him. John 7:37 states, "Now on the last day, the great day of the feast, Jesus stood and cried out,

saying, 'If any man is thirsty, let him come to Me and drink.'"
The principle here is only the thirsty get invited to drink.
Therefore, God has to let something into your life labeled
"dry times" that will stimulate your thirst so you can then
receive an invitation by the Spirit to partake of the water
from a fresh river of life.

The second reason is to motivate you to look for water in places where your tradition and legalism have kept
you from exploring. That is why the pool doesn't appear in
your dry times until they become scorched. When you get
that thirsty, you won't care where the water comes from. If
it is wet, you will drink it. Proverbs 27:7 states, "To a fam-
ished man any bitter thing is sweet." In the late 1960s and
early 1970s, the Charismatic Renewal came into existence
because a lot of Christians in traditional churches got so
thirsty that they were willing to drink from the pool of the
"baptism in the Holy Spirit"—even though it included controversy and ridicule from family and friends.

LARRY

Let me give you an example from my own life of how
a "scorched land became a pool" and how the "pool" itself
was one I normally wouldn't drink from. When I was first
put into prison, I stayed away from the other inmates because
of fear and mistrust. After a while, I realized that if I was going to grow in my Christian faith, I was going to need the
interactions of other believers. Not really knowing who was
or wasn't a believer, I started praying and asking God to send
me someone who could help me grow in my Christianity.
After a month of praying with no answer in sight, my prayer
changed from "send me somebody" to "send me anybody."

God waited until my thirst was sufficiently stimulated
before He sent me the person who could most help me to
grow. Had he sent this person prior to my prayer changing from "somebody" to "anybody," I would have rejected
him. The person He sent was the last person in the prison
I would have chosen for the role. The person He sent was
named Larry. I didn't know Larry very well but what I did
know caused me to keep my distance from him. He was one

of the biggest drug dealers in the prison and was one of the weirdest people I had ever met. He was also someone who persecuted and mocked me because of my Christianity. So, you would understand my surprise when he showed up at my bunk one day and asked me if he could talk to me.

He told me that he had just gotten out of the "hole," which is the inner jail in the prison. He went on to tell me that while he was there, he has surrendered his life to Christ. Now that he was out, he wanted to get with other Christians in order to grow in his faith. Since I was the only Christian he knew, he came to me. Though I was a little suspicious of his real motives, I received him as the answer to my prayer. I even got my bunk moved next to his. After about a week of trying to relate to this man, I was praying "Lord, take him back." I thought the Lord was going to bring me some-body who would both encourage and inspire me, somebody who would help me know what loving someone is all about. Larry was moody, sarcastic, and an excessive talker and my time with him was both discouraging and depressing. Instead of knowing what love is, I was beginning to experience hate in ways I had never known.

As I began to pray about my relationship with Larry, God brought to memory a fairy tale I had learned as a child. It was the tale of how a beautiful Princess stooped down and kissed an ugly little toad and as a result of the kiss, the ugly toad was transformed into a handsome Prince Charming. As I meditated on this, God showed me that there is an ugly toad in all of us. I began to realize that the only thing pow-erful enough to transform something ugly into something beautiful is love. All of us need someone to love us just the way we are, ugly toad and all, if we are ever going to be transformed into that beautiful person God created us to be. The things in Larry I considered ugly would always stay that way until somebody was willing to love him in spite of them.

Armed with this revelation, I received Larry as the an-swer to my prayer. When he was moody, I loved him. When he got sarcastic, I loved him even more. When he wouldn't shut up, I loved him by listening to him. Slowly but surely, he was transformed into the kind of friend I had been looking

for all my life. And by the way, the toad in me was transformed into a prince because Larry decided to love me just
the way I was, warts and all. Initially Larry was a scorched
land for me, but ultimately he became one of the most life
refreshing pools from which I had ever taken a drink.

I came to understand that "dry times" are for promotion and not punishment. This is important because the
enemy will point out some sin in your life as the reason for
your dry time. He will say it's because you not been having consistent quiet times, or you're not tithing enough, or
you're failing as a parent and these are the reasons for your
"scorched land." However, Psalm 103:10 states, "He hath not
dealt with us after our sins; nor does He treat us the way our
sins deserve." When God deal with us, sin usually isn't the
issue for it has been removed for verse 12 goes on the say,
*"as far as the east is from the west, so far has He removed our trans-
gressions from us."* Therefore, His dealings aren't punishment
for your sin, but for the production of your soul; He's not
condemning you for how you are, but seeking to conform
you to the person He created you to be; He is not so much
pointing out a weakness, as He is seeking to pour in His
strength; and He's not denouncing your flaws, but wanting
to develop your faith. In your dry times, the enemy will try
and get you to focus on fixing a problem instead of finding
a pool.

The second phrase is found in Verse 8: *"And a highway
will be there."* The Hebrew word translated *highway* is *macluwl*
which means *a thoroughfare, path or journey.* Just like there is a
pool in the midst of the scorched land, there is also a path in
the midst of the pool. Where dry times are designed to stimulate our thirst, drinking is designed to give us a direction.
All drinking is to strengthen and refresh us so God can take
us on a journey. In Acts 2, the "Upper Room experience" of
receiving the Holy Spirit was for the "in all the world pro-
claiming" of the gospel. In Acts 10, Peter's "roof top vision"
was for his "room full of Gentiles testimony."

We can see this same dynamic in John 13, but instead
of thirst, hunger is the condition described. John 13:4-5 states
"that Jesus rose from supper and laid aside His garments,

took a towel and girded Himself. After that, He poured water into a basin and began to wash the disciples' feet, and to wipe them with the towel with which He was girded" (NKJV). In a sense, Jesus went from "supper time to service time." He understood that the meal was designed to energize Him for service, that one shouldn't eat primarily for pleasure but for productivity. It's my belief that not only is there direction into His purpose when we drink from His pool, but also after every spiritual meal the Lord gives us, there is a towel of service with which He wants us to gird ourselves.

The third phrase is also found in verse 8 and is "and a roadway." The Hebrew word for *roadway* is *derek,* which means *a course of life or destiny.* The implication is that your drinking will help you find the direction to your destiny. Your destiny is what God had in mind when He created you. You were not only saved from something, but you were also saved for something. Most of us, when we think of sin, we think of the branches of sin and not the root. In Romans 3:23, Paul wrote, "for all have sinned and fall short of the glory of God." The Greek word translated *sinned* is the word *hamartano,* which simply means *to miss the mark.*

The implication is that God has a mark for us to hit in this life. This allows the Lord to do through us what He has done in us. Anything that keeps us from doing that is sin. Obviously indulging self through lust, lies, theft, or murder will keep us from not only hitting the mark, but even knowing there is a mark. However, there is another form of indulging self that is more subtle. It's where we give into fears, insensitivity, inconsideration, or lack of compassion that causes us not even to attempt to aim for the mark. Biblical sin has more to do with not doing the things that you should than it does with doing the things you shouldn't. James 4:17 says, "Anyone, then, who knows the good he ought to do and doesn't do it, sins." True repentance is not only turning away from something that is wrong, but is also turning towards something that is right.

"Wisdom is the principal thing; therefore get wisdom: and with all thy getting get understanding" (Proverbs 4:7 KJV). We have become great "getters." We "get" saved, filled, delivered, healed, blessed, etc. Perhaps you have developed the art of *spending God*. With all of your getting, are you walking in defeat? Do you let Satan get the best of you? Why haven't you impacted the world the way you know that you can and should. The reason for this could be that "with all of your getting, you haven't gotten understanding." It is one thing to know Jesus will save you and fix you up, but it is another to know why He does it.

Jesus saved you and fixed you up for a purpose. Jesus not only saved you *from* something, He also saved you *for* something. All He has done for you, all He has given you, and all He has allowed you to go through were for a reason. He had a purpose in mind. To this end you need to cry out for understanding, because to miss the purpose for which the Lord has done all of this is to miss living the abundant life Jesus promised. The abundance of life is more about who you are and what you do than it is about what you have.

In Ephesians 2:10 Paul stated, "For you are His workmanship, created in Christ Jesus for good works" (NASB). There are two phrases in this verse that I would like to address so you will have a better understanding of what God is after in your life. The first is found in the phrase "you are His workmanship." Paul was communicating that God is the one who created you, and He used great skill in doing so. As a master craftsman, He took great care in what He was doing because you were going to be a "masterpiece."

Psalm 139:13-16 describes the skill with which the Lord put you together and how He is concerned about every detail of your life. He was the one that gave you your individual physical features, your personality, and your different capacities for feeling, thinking, and sensing. It's no accident you are unique and different from everyone else. There has never been anyone like you. There isn't anyone like you now and there will never be anyone quite like you in the future. You have a unique expression of God that the world needs to see and touch.

God had a purpose in creating you. In fact, before you were, your purpose was and your purpose determined how you were going to be. Just like the job determines the design of the tool, so does God's purpose determine the design of the person. God looked down the corridor of time and saw something (a destiny) that needed to be fulfilled and He created you with that in mind. He said in order for you to fulfill your destiny, you will need this type of personality, this level of intelligence, this perspective, this sense of humor, etc. God designed you with everything you need to successfully attain your destiny.

The second phrase is "you were created in Christ Jesus for good works." The Greek word translated *good* in this verse is *agathos*, which means *to excel in something and be useful*. Again, we see that God created us to be useful in some way. In Colossians 1:28, Paul goes on to say, "We preach Him, warning every man and teaching every man in all wisdom, that we may present every man perfect in Christ Jesus" (NKJV). The Greek word translated perfect is *teleios* meaning *to bring something to its end or completion*. In fact, other translations use the word *complete* instead of *perfect*.

One of the ideas behind this word is to be completed by the purpose for which God created you. It has the imagery of aligning the right tool (you) with the right job (God's purpose). For example, the perfect tool for putting a nail into a board would be a hammer. The hammer was specifically design for this job. When the head of the hammer hits the head of the nail, it is a perfect fit, for it was to this end that the hammer was made. And when God aligns you with the destiny for which you were created, it is perfect. You are not only perfect for it, but it is perfect for you. Paul further gave evidence of this when he wrote in Philippians 3:12, "Not that I have already obtained it, or have already become perfect, but I press on in order that I may lay hold of that for which also I was laid hold of by Christ Jesus" (NASB). For Paul, perfection meant "laying hold of that for which he was laid hold of for."

What you need to understand is that since coming to Jesus, everything we have been given and gone through was to prepare us for the purpose God has for our lives. King David understood this principle and spent his life in the pursuit of the goal of fulfilling God's purpose for his life.

Acts 13:36 tells us he achieved this goal, "For David, after he served the purpose of God in his own generation, fell asleep."

In the movie *Chariots of Fire*, there is a scene in which Eric Liddell, a Scottish runner, had just run a successful race and then held a successful evangelistic meeting after the race. His sister was trying to get him to quit running and go into full-time ministry. He responded to her by saying, "But God has made me fast, and when I run, I feel His pleasure." Eric realized that He was fast for a purpose and when he was fulfilling that purpose, he felt God's pleasure. The question you need to answer is what has God made you fast to do. By that, I mean what area of life do you excel in? It may be in serving, organizing, speaking, writing, singing, or a host of other activities. What is it that when you do it, you feel His pleasure?

For me, the answer to that question is prison ministry. I excel in prison ministry more than in any other aspect of ministry and when I am conducting ministry in a prison, I feel His pleasure. Not only am I the perfect tool for it, but it is the perfect job for me. You can always tell what your destiny is because it is something that won't drain or deplete you, but it is something that will delight and develop you. Around my house, whenever I get a little grumpy and critical, one of my children will always say to me, "Dad, can't you find a prison to preach in?" They have learned that after I am finished with prison ministry, I am good to go and my grumpiness has been replaced by happiness and my criticism has been replaced by optimism.

Matthew 7:13-14 says, "You can enter God's Kingdom only through the narrow gate. The highway to hell is broad, and its gate is wide for the many who choose the easy way. But the gateway to life is small, and the road is narrow, and only a few ever find it" (NLT). In the context of realizing that God has made us for a purpose, what does being narrow mean? *Noah Webster's 1828 Dictionary* defines narrow this way: *of little breadth; not wide or broad; very limited*. In our day it has become a negative word, one that few people want to be associated with. We often hear it used in a condemning way. When we say someone is narrow, we most often mean that they are one-sided, not open-minded, not fully grown; or is dwarfed and defective in some way. Jesus was someone who was narrow, but He was in no way narrow in the sense I just described.

When Jesus talked to men about the two ways, one of them narrow and the other one broad, He was speaking out of His own experience. He was narrow in that He set definite boundaries for Himself and shut Himself up within certain limitations.

> By standing in one place and striking repeatedly the strings of the same set of hearts, He started vibrations which have filled the world with music. By carefully tending the fire which He had kindled, He made it hot enough to change the spiritual climate of the whole world. By saturating a little circle of chosen followers with His Spirit, He made them capable of carrying on their shoulders a lost race to God. By persistently treading a single path, He made that path so luminous that every eye can see it. By being faithful in a few things, He won the place of Lordship over all things (Charles-Edward Jefferson, *Jesus The Same*, page 87).

In the same way, it's only when we give ourselves to His purpose and our destiny and say, "Inside of this sphere I purpose to do my work," that real life begins and our heart learns the art of singing. It is when we pick up in our hand a definite, tiny task and say, "This is the thing to which I shall devote my life," the shadows vanish and life becomes worth living. It is that narrow path that leads to life. If you want to see someone who sings at their work, look for them inside a narrow circle.

Being narrow will cause the light that God has given to us to become focused. Focused light has tremendous power while diffused light has no power at all. For instance, by focusing the power of the sun through a magnifying glass, you can set a leaf on fire. When light is concentrated at a more intense level, like a laser beam, it can even cut through a block of steel. The principle of concentration works in other areas, too. The focused life will have a far greater impact than an unfocused one. Like a laser beam, the more focused we are, the more impact we will have on society. Paul wrote in Philippians 3:13, "I am bringing all my energies to bear on this one thing, forgetting what is behind and looking for to what lies ahead" (TLB). If our time and energy are diffused and dissipated, then the power that comes only through purpose is lost. Just as Jesus became mighty by limiting Himself, we can too.

The fourth and final phrase is found in verse 8 as well, "it will be called the way of holiness." The implication is that your destiny is what will bring holiness to your life. The Hebrew word translated *holiness* is *qodesh*, which means *separated or consecrated to God's service*. In one sense, holiness has more to do with vocation than it does condition. Let me explain what I mean.

One Christmas my uncle gave me a stainless steel cup from Starbucks as a present but I only use this cup for hot chocolate. In my house it is a sin (which means to miss the mark) to use this cup for anything other than hot chocolate, for it has been set aside and consecrated for that particular service. When I am sipping hot chocolate from it, it is in the truest sense of the word *holy*. In fact, if my cup had feelings, it would sense my pleasure of the service it was doing.

Your destiny is the way to holiness which is determined by your purpose, not your purity. It is when you pursue your purpose that you will be motivated to produce your purity. A lot of Christians miss their purpose because they are waiting until they are pure enough to pursue it. Their thinking is they have to quit messing up before they are able to minister, when in reality if they would just go ahead and minister, they would quit messing up. A lot of people take the posture that says, "I have to quit fulfilling the lust of the flesh before I can walk in the Spirit." However, Paul told us in Galatians 5:16 to "walk in the Spirit, and you shall not fulfil the lust of the flesh" (KJV). In other words, the power not to do the things we shouldn't is generated when we start doing the things we should. God doesn't call the qualified, He qualifies the called.

Once you sense His pleasure with the service you are producing, you will deal with anything that will disqualify you for that service. Paul put it this way in 1 Corinthians 9:27: "I buffet my body and make it my slave, lest possibly, after I have preached to others, I myself should be disqualified." Hebrews 12:1 states it this way: "Let us lay aside every encumbrance, and the sin which so easily entangles us, and let us run with endurance the race that is set before us." The joy found in running the race will cause you to deal with anything that will hinder or entangle you.

In 1 Corinthians 16:9, Paul explained that "a wide and effective door of service has been opened to me, but there are many adversaries." Paul understood that with increased opportunity comes increased opposition. Therefore, as a minister I face a lot of perils and pitfalls. I have found that the enemy doesn't attack the work of God, but the worker for God. He will attack the things that interest me in order to take my eyes off the things that interest God. What motivates me to deal with sin, fight the temptation, make the sacrifices is that I don't want anything to keep me from the purpose that brings me His pleasure.

Everything I just wrote can be summed up in this truth. Dry times will cause you to want to drink, as you drink you will find a direction, as you pursue that direction you will find a destiny, and as you fulfill your destiny you will be motivated to bring much needed discipline to the entirety of your life.

THIRTEEN

A DENT IN YOUR ARMOR DOESN'T DISQUALIFY YOU FOR THE BATTLE

God's way of using our failures to produce His successes

Let me start this chapter with an interesting if quite old story from the world of college football:

On New Year's Day, 1929, Georgia Tech played University of California in the Rose Bowl. In that game a man named Roy Riegels recovered a fumble for California. Somehow, he became confused and started running in the wrong direction. One of his teammates, overtook and downed him sixty-five yards away, just before he scored for the opposing team. That strange play came in the first half, and everyone who was watching the game was asking the same question: 'What will Coach Price do with Roy in the second half?' The men filed off the field and went into the dressing room.

They sat down on the benches and on the floor, all but Riegels. He put his blanket around his shoulders, sat down in a corner, put his face in his hands, and cried like a baby. When the timekeeper came in and announced that there were three minutes before playing time. Coach Price looked at the team and said simply, 'Men, the same team that played the first half will start the second.' The players got up and started out, all but Riegels. He did not budge. The coach looked back and called to him. Still he didn't move. Coach Price went over to where Riegels sat and said, 'Roy, didn't you hear me? The same team that played the first half will start the second.' Then Riegels looked up and his cheeks were wet with a strong man's tears. 'Coach,' he said, 'I can't do it to save my life. I've ruined you. I've ruined the University of California. I've ruined myself. I couldn't face that crowd in the stadium to save my life. Then Coach Price reached out and put his hand on Riegels' shoulder and said to him: 'Son, you made a bad play, but you are not a bad player, get up and go on back; the game is only half over.' And Riegels went back. Those Tech men will tell you they have never seen a man play football as Roy played that second half (*The New York Times*, http://archive. nytimes.com/www.nytimes.com/packages/html/ sports/year_in_sports/01.01.html).

I don't know about you, but at times I have taken the ball morally, relationally, and spiritually and run in the wrong direction, unfortunately scoring points for the other side. We all stumble and fall, which results in being ashamed of ourselves and the desire never to try again. However, it is at these moments that God comes and bends over us, in the person of His Son, and says, "Son or daughter, you made a bad decision, but you're not a bad person, therefore get up and go on back; the game is only half over." That is the gospel of the grace of God. It is the gospel of a second chance, of a third chance, of the hundredth chance.

Many years ago, I was channel surfing trying to find something worthwhile to watch. As I did, I came upon the Oprah Winfrey Show, and normally I would keep surfing, but I just happened to land on it when Oprah was asking Elizabeth Taylor why she was getting married again. This piqued my curiosity, knowing that she had been married several times, so I stopped to listen to this dialogue. Oprah asked "Why are you getting married again? This will be your eighth marriage. None of the others worked out, so why don't you just live with this man, and save yourself and him a lot of heartache and expense." Elizabeth responded with an astounding answer: "Just because I'm not good at being married, doesn't mean I don't believe in the institution of marriage."

I could relate to her answer, for I haven't always been good at being a Christian, but since the day I met Jesus, I have wholeheartedly believed in Christianity. Though I lie on occasion, I am not a liar. Though I fail on occasion, I am not a failure. Though I am fearful on occasion, I am not a coward. I have made some bad plays as a Christian, but I am not a bad player. I am who God created and saved me to be. The enemy wants us to view our lives through episodes of failure, while the Lord wants us to view our lives through His eternal victory. I will not let momentary incidents determine my infinite standing with God, and neither should you.

One of the hardest things, I have had to grapple with as a Christian is believing there is a holy God in heaven who loves me just the way I am. He loves me when I am up, and loves me when I am down. He loves me when I succeed, and loves me when I fail. He loves me when I do right, and who loves me when I do wrong.

The apostle John also grappled with this and shared his conclusion with us in 1 John 4:16: "And we have come to know and have believed the love which God has for us." The Greek word translated *come to know* is *ginosko,* which means a *slow dawning or gradual realization*. It is knowing by experiencing. It implies that this is a process, and it will take more than one demonstration of His love to convince us. Paul wrote in Ephesians 3:18 and confirmed this truth: "That you may be able to comprehend with all the saints what is the breadth and length and height and depth, and to know the love of Christ which surpasses knowledge."The Greek word translated *comprehend* is *katalambano,* which means *to lay hold of or take possession of.* It is the same word used in Philippians 3 where Paul's wrote, "I want to apprehend that which I have been apprehended for." It is the same word used in Acts 10:34 when Peter said, "Now I understand." The implication is that God takes us through things so that we can comprehend and apprehend His love both for ourselves and others.

This process usually involves failure which is the reason Paul wrote about the "breadth, length, height and depth of God's love." When we fail others, His love is wide and long enough to cover it. When we fail ourselves, His love is again deep enough to cover it. And when we fail God, His love is high enough to cover it. Romans 8:31-39 gives us four "who's" and seventeen "what's" that cannot separate us from the love of God:

> What then shall we say to these things? If God is for us, who can be against us? He who did not spare his own Son but gave him up for us all, how will he not also with him graciously give us all things? Who shall bring any charge against God's elect? It is God who justifies. Who is to condemn? Christ Jesus is the one who died—more than that, who was raised—who is at the right hand of God, who indeed is interceding for us. Who shall separate us from the love of Christ? Shall tribulation, or distress, or persecution, or famine, or nakedness, or danger, or sword? As it is written, 'for your sake we are being killed all the day long; we are regarded as sheep to be slaughtered.' No, in all these things we are more than conquerors through him who loved us. For I am sure that neither death nor life, nor angels nor rulers, nor things present nor things to come, nor powers, nor height nor depth, nor anything else in all creation, will be able to

separate us from the love of God in Christ Jesus our Lord."

Most of us know and believe that nothing in our past before meeting Christ can separate us from His love. Therefore, our struggle isn't with pre-conversion sin, but post-conversion sin. Verse 38 tells us that neither can anything in our "present" or our "future" separate us from His love.

It is important that once you have made Jesus Savior of your soul, you then make Him Lord of your life. The first should always produce the latter. Once you comprehend His love, you will willingly apprehend His Lordship. This was demonstrated in my own life on July 26, 1972 when I surrendered my heart to His love, and the next day I turned myself into the authorities, thereby apprehending His Lordship. If you don't, then "God's grace" that produces "second chances," becomes "cheap grace" and produces "sickly Christians."

Jesus said in John 15:16, "You did not choose Me, but I chose you, and appointed you, that you should go and bear fruit, and that your fruit should remain, that whatever you ask of the Father in My name, He may give to you" (NAS). A heart-breaking aspect of ministry is to bear fruit only to find out later that it didn't remain. It's hard and discouraging to see men and women you have given your life to, in the hope they will meet the Lord and make the changes that will free them and make them productive people, return to their old ways.

The main reason this happens is because people want to be free from the consequences of their sin more than they want to be free from the actual sin. They turn to God in order to escape the consequences of their actions instead of looking to God for forgiveness of their sin so they can find the strength to face those consequences. This kind of religion is called "cheap grace," and is motivated by self-preservation, whereas true conversion is motivated by a transformation of self.

As I wrote earlier, comprehending His love will cause you to apprehend His Lordship, which will then free you to become what I call a "believable believer." A lot of Christians have a hard time being real with their Christianity because many are not comfortable with their humanity. Therefore, they come across as being more than they really are or having more than they really do. It is hard to take an ordinary man, from an ordinary background, and tell him he must be "god-like." It's a real challenge to be real with our humanity, while seeking to be conformed to His image.

An example of this can be found in the life of Peter. In Matthew 16:16, we read Peter's response to a question Jesus asked: "Who do men say that I am?" was Spirit-inspired: "You are the Christ the Son of God." But just six verses later, Peter rebuked the Lord with a devil-inspired admonishment. He demonstrated faith by walking on water, but then succumbed to fear and sank. He acted courageously in front of the soldiers who came to arrest Jesus, and yet a few hours later acted like a coward in front of a servant girl. He went from flowing to failing to flowing to failing to flowing to failing. The thing that caused Peter to keep getting back up after he failed was his understanding that following Jesus was not about a mandate to be perfect, but a means to be perfected. Peter understood that the "gospel of the eternal second chance" afforded him the opportunity to become what I call a "believable believer."

One of the reasons the Bible is such a great book is because we can relate to it. No other holy book paints its characters with such honesty. The followers of God in the Bible were not perfect, but they were powerful. Consider the following: Noah got drunk and naked in his own tent; Abraham lying and putting his wife at risk of rape to save himself; Lot having an incestuous relationship with his daughter; Moses murdering an Egyptian to prove that God sent him; Aaron doing fireside aerobics in front of a golden calf; David committing adultery and then murder to cover it; Peter, the rock, denying and cussing before a frail servant girl; and Paul the Apostle, who referred to himself as the "chief of sinners" and yet we continually eat a perfect Word from his stained hands. They were not superhuman, but they were revelatory. They were often chastised and corrected, but they were never discarded.

Hebrews 11 contains a list of the heroes of faith, but the Scriptures clearly state that these heroes were made strong out of weakness. Look at the men mentioned in verses 32–34 and reflect on their lives. They were not glaring examples of flawless character; yet they epitomized faith toward God. Gideon failed by requesting a sign. Barak wouldn't go into battle unless the queen went with him. Samson shined on the battlefield, but had struggles in the bedroom. Jephthah made a foolish and destructive vow. We must be careful when judging the weak moments in their lives as we consider the entirety of their lives. If we do, we will see that a dent in their armor did not disqualify them for the battle.

Isn't a hero someone who puts himself at risk to help someone else? I have found that anybody who is doing anything for the Lord has a bull's eye on his or her life and the more he or she is doing, the bigger the bull's eye gets. First Corinthians 16:9 says, "For a wide door for effective service has opened to me, and there are many adversaries." Paul understood that you can't separate the "wide effective door of service" from "the many adversaries." Increased opportunities always bring increased oppositions. Hebrews 10:32 speaks to this concept when the writer said, "But remember the former days, when, after being enlightened, you endured a great conflict of sufferings."

The writer understood that after God enlightens you in some way, you will then have to endure a conflict. You need to get used to the fact that the fire of God will always bring a fight for God, that a burden will always bring a battle. The reason this happens is the light that shines in darkness will also show up in darkness. Both sinners and Satan will be drawn to the light, sinners to be healed by it while Satan to try and put it out. But if you "endure the conflict," God will use the fight to make you fit, and He will use the battle to make you better. I wonder if some of the men and women whom we say "failed" actually tarnished their records by having the courage to climb high enough to take risks some were not willing to take to help others. I am not glamorizing or condoning sin. Sin is a stench in God's nostrils, but have our noses become more sensitive than God's?

Hebrews 12:15 gives us instructions for how to deal with people in our midst who have failed: "Look out for each other so that none of you will miss out on the special favor of God's grace. Watch out that no bitter root of unbelief rises up among you, for whenever it springs up, many are corrupted by its poison" (NLT). In this passage there are two phrases that I would like to look at more closely: "look out" and "watch out."

Let's look first at "look out." The Greek word for *look out* is *episkopoo,* which means *to look upon others in such a way that you are inspecting their lives for the purpose of caring for them.* The inspection here is to keep them from falling short or lacking in some area life. It's not for the purpose of judging how they are, but for the purpose of encouraging them to become what they should be. We are told to *look* for the ones who are *missing out.* The Greek word translated *miss out* is *husteroo,* which means *to be inferior, to fail, be lacking, and to be in want.* It's telling us to "look out" for the ones in our midst who have failed and as a result are in want in some area of their life. It is the same word translated "hurt" in the story of the prodigal son, which states, "There, undisciplined and dissipated, he wasted everything he had. After he had gone through all his money he began to hurt" (Luke 15:13-14 MSG). This hurt was a result of the son's own sinful actions and in a sense he was getting what he deserved. That wasn't the posture of the prodigal's father and it's not the posture of our Father, so it can't be our posture.

The implication is that the ones who are messing up are also missing out because of something wrong they are doing. In this verse, God is telling us that the right thing to do is to make sure they don't miss out. In other words, we need to look out for those who are in trouble because of some sin in their lives. Once we discover who these "messer uppers" are, we then need to bestow the grace of God on their lives. We are not to treat them the way their sins deserve but treat them the way the Son deserves.

Our actions shouldn't be to condemn people for how they are, but seek to conform them in how they should be. It's not our job to bring punishment to their sin but to bring production to their soul. This can be difficult for us because our human propensity is to judge their sin instead of loving their soul. We want to point out a weakness, instead of pouring in His strength. We want to denounce their flaws, instead of developing their faith. We want to criticize their failings, instead of caring for their future. We want to condemn their habits, instead of comforting their hurts. We want to be fruit inspectors, instead of fruit cultivators.

FIVE IMPORTANT WORDS

Greed brings messes but grace brings mending. In Romans 2:4, there are five words that will give us insight that will not only help us understand the power of God's grace, but also how to apply it to those who are in need of it. The verse reads, "Or do you think lightly of the riches of His kindness and forbearance and longsuffering, not knowing that the kindness of God leads you to repentance?" (NASB).

The first word is *think lightly*. The Greek word is *katafronoo*, which means *to despise, disesteem, discount, disdain, or think little of.* The literal meaning is to think that something has no value. Paul was admonishing us not to undervalue the power of an act of kindness. That brings to our second word, *kindness* or the Greek word *chrestotes,* which means *an event or action that is useful and benevolent.* Benevolence is defined as "a desire to promote prosperity and happiness at no cost." It signifies not merely goodness as a quality, but instead goodness in action, expressing itself in deeds. It is the same word translated as *gentleness* in Galatians 5:22 as one of the fruit of the spirit. This means God wants us to be as kind to others as He has been to us.

In trying to help those who are hurting, some people mean well, but their meanness is greater than their wellness. In 1984 when my wife and I had a baby born stillborn, a friend of ours who was also a Christian called us and told us that if we had faith God would raise our baby from the dead. He meant well but his words were neither kind nor helpful. Cultivating kindness should be an important parts of our lives. We need to train our hearts to give kindness and our hands to give help. Kindness offers whatever is necessary to heal the hurts of others. Kindness has converted more sinners than either zeal, eloquence, or learning, so therefore we can't afford to "think lightly" of it.

The third word is *forbearance*. The Greek word is *anoche* which means *a delay or suspension of punishment in order for repentance to be worked out*. It means you have to suspend your hatred of their sin so you can bring some healing to their soul. It is a putting up with what you don't like until what you do like comes forth. It's worth noting that Jesus didn't condemn bad people. He condemned "stiff" people. We tend to do the opposite and condemn the bad ones while affirming the stiff ones. Whether it was a prostitute or a tax collector or an outcast, Jesus reached out to them. A motley crew of riffraff followed Him around, but it never embarrassed Him or made Him feel uncomfortable.

The fourth word is *longsuffering* for which the Greek word is *makrothumia*. This means *a state of emotional calm in the face of provocation*. It also means *a slowness in avenging a wrong done to you*. It is self-restraint in the face of injury, which does not hastily retaliate or promptly punish. The implication is that as you seek to help those who are hurting, they in all likelihood will inflict hurt on you.

There is a story told of a man who loved animals. As he was driving home from work one night, he noticed a squirrel on the side of the road that had been injured. Realizing he would drive right by an animal hospital, he decided he would take the squirrel there. Unfortunately, when he went to pick it up, the squirrel bit him. In his pain the man threw the squirrel to the ground and kicked it, because being hurt caused him to lose sight of his mission to bring help. This is indicative of what happens to us when we get involved in the lives of those who are hurting. Often the very people we are trying to help will hurt us, but unlike the man with the squirrel, we can't afford to let the hurt keep us from our mission to bring healing to the hurt they are experiencing.

The fifth and final word is *leadeth*. The Greek word is *ago,* which means to carry or accompany. Notice that this verse doesn't say that they immediately repent, but they are being led to repentance. The idea is that our kindness will carry, support, and minister to people until they can repent. A lot of my fellow Christians have the attitude that as soon as they repent, then we will be kind. This verse tells us to go ahead and be kind and they will repent. Romans 12:21 admonishes us to not "let evil get the best of you; get the best of evil by doing good." The only thing powerful enough to overcome evil is good so when someone does you wrong, you can overcome them by doing them right and being kind. We overcome them not by defeating them but by winning them.

It takes the whole package in order to bring someone to repentance. First, we esteem, count on, and think highly of God's kindness, realizing what kind of effect this kindness had on us. That should then spur us to action on behalf of others. Then we will have to delay and suspend our judgments over their past actions. We will have to restrain ourselves from retaliating when their continued actions provoke and injure us. We will do this knowing that each act of kindness, forbearance, and longsuffering is releasing power and is moving the one who has fallen short of the grace God one step closer to the day he or she repents.

If we look back at Hebrew 12:15, the second phrase of note is "*Watch out* that no bitter root of unbelief rises up among you, for whenever it springs up, many are corrupted by its poison." Where the phrase *look out* implied action that needs to be taken, the phrase *watch out* implies actions that needed to be avoided. In other words, after you look out for the individual who is in need of God's grace, you need to watch out for the ones who don't believe the individual should have gotten it, for when God blesses someone they don't believe deserved it, they can become bitter.

This is especially true when God uses a human instrument to do the blessing because they can then justify their bitterness by accusing the blesser as being deceived. When that happens, they become bitter not only at the one being blessed but also at the one who is doing the blessing. You can see this dynamic in the story of the prodigal son. The father was looking out for the son who needed grace, then he had to watch out for the son who got bitter because the prodigal got blessed. Who are the ones that we need to "watch out" for? They are the ones who refused to "look out" for the ones who needed some grace. A heart that doesn't easily allow grace to spring forth from it is a heart that easily allows a bitter root to grow out of it.

Although we don't have to be perfect, we must be people who are resilient enough to survive tragedy and adversity. If you don't survive, you can't save someone else from it. We need to live long enough to invest the wealth of our experience in the release of some other victim whom Satan desires to bind or incapacitate as Paul reminded us in 2 Corinthians 1:3-4: "Blessed be the God and Father of our Lord Jesus Christ, the Father of mercies and God of all comfort; who comforts us in all our affliction so that we may be able to comfort those who are in any affliction with the comfort with which we ourselves are comforted by God."

God has a different definition of peace and safety than we do. To be wounded in the fight is a great honor. It is by the Lord's stripes that we are healed, and it is through our stripes that we also are given the authority for healing. In the very place that the enemy wounds us, we are given the power to heal others once we are healed. The Lord allows bad things to happen to His people, so they can receive the compassion for others by which the power of healing operates. Every bad thing that happens to us can be turned into the authority to do good. Because of Jesus, I was able to survive drug addiction, alcoholism and a 30-year prison sentence. As a result, I now have the compassion, authority, and power to bring healing and deliverance to drug addicts, alcoholics, and convicts.

I can't help but wonder if we have forsaken some of God's finest people when they came under attack and failed. They could bring us a voice from the graveyard of failure expressing the truth that there is life after death. Revival must start in the trash can of our churches and community even though in ignorance and religious pride we have sometimes discarded what God has regarded. We need to remember that God is still in the business of recycling human lives. It's not every day that we find someone who will give someone a second chance, let alone someone who will give *you* a second chance every day. In Christ and His gospel we have both.

I'm afraid we sometimes destroy our heroes because we were looking for the superhuman and perfect. It's time for us to redefine and redirect our gaze to find the heroes of God among us. We must never forget that God purposely chooses to use misplaced and rejected people. Who knows, God may be looking in your direction.

FOURTEEN

TOTAL TRUST IN GOD

God's way of using the sickness in my body to bring healing to my soul

This is the written testimony of the fact that God healed me of a life-threatening disease in 2006. I initially titled this chapter "testimony of how God healed me," but I realized that would be presumptuous of me to try and instruct others on the "how" of anything that pertains to God. As much as I would like to think I had something to do with this healing, I have to admit right at the beginning that if the healing depended on anything I said or did, I would still be sick. During this process, I can't tell you about any great faith I expressed. Most of my prayers were like the father of the boy who couldn't speak in Mark 9, "I believe, but please help me with my unbelief."

God didn't heal me because I am a good person because I'm not. I've realized over the years the more light I receive from God, the more darkness is revealed in my life. Every day, I need His mercy and grace for not only the sins I commit, but also for the righteousness I attempt, for it consistently falls short of the righteousness God requires. It is this same mercy and grace which released His miracle-working power and brought healing to my body.

The Christian life more often than leaves us in a quandary. Probing and disturbing questions far outnumber absolute and air-tight answers. The more we try to mine the knowledge of God, the more we realize how little we know. This is especially true in the area of human suffering caused by physical sickness. Healing, like most things of God, is shrouded in mystery so it is imperative that we learn to respect the mystery. If you are hoping for a formula you can apply to your life to ensure God will heal you as well, you might as well stop reading now, for God and His ways can never be reduced to a formula. Real faith cannot be reduced to a spiritual three-step process and merchandised as success stories. Real faith is refined in the fires and storms of life.

My father in the Lord, Charles Simpson, once said concerning God's power, "We can never make anything happen, but we can make room for it to happen." In other words, there are things we can do to position ourselves to receive God's grace. This testimony is not just about how I got sick and then God healed me. It's more about how God used the sickness of my body to bring healing to my soul. The miracle I want to testify about isn't just what God did for me, but also what He has done in me through this whole ordeal. I don't know why God healed me while choosing not to heal others. All I can do is offer you my story and hope it will ignite faith in you to embrace your particular storm, be educated by it, and then finally be extricated from it by an all-loving and powerful God.

THE TRIAL

In December 2005, I received a phone call from my best friend, Jim Britnell, who lived in Pensacola, Florida. He was calling me to tell me that he just got back from the doctor's office where he found out his blood work from a few weeks earlier indicated he had tested positive for the Hepatitis C virus. He also informed me he had a viral load of 173,000, which was high and can be life threatening. He told me I should get tested because people who were in prison are considered a high-risk group.

Before I go any further, let me tell you a little about this virus. It is in the same family as the AIDS virus, both incurable and potentially lethal. Whereas the AIDS virus attacks the immune system, the Hep C virus attacks the liver. Unlike AIDS, the Hep C virus doesn't spread through immoral behavior but can only be contracted by blood-to-blood contact. It is known as the "silent killer" because a lot of people exhibit no symptoms up until the day their liver ceases to function and they die.

After I got off the phone with my friend, I called my family doctor to make an appointment to get the necessary blood work done. In January, while I was on a ministry trip, I received a call from my family doctor informing me that the blood work results were back and I had tested positive for the Hep C virus. He also informed me that my viral load was 10,600,000. He sent me to a Hep C specialist for further testing. The subsequent testing indicated I had severe liver damage. The tests showed I had an alarming amount of fat and a dangerous amount of iron in my liver along with a dangerous amount of ammonia in my blood. I also had damage on the cellular level; I had scarring on my liver; my liver was enlarged as were some of the organs attached to it. All this indicated that I was at the fourth and final stage of liver damage, known as cirrhosis of the liver. The doctor told me I had anywhere between two and five years before my liver would fail, at which point I would need a liver transplant or die.

As you might expect, this was devastating news to me and my family. I was 55 years old and had always enjoyed excellent health. I have never taken medication on a regular basis, and it was rare for me to even get a cold. But there I was, not only sick, but with an incurable disease that could end my life within a couple of years. When I got back from the doctors, I sat my family down and broke the news to them. After many tears, we began to pray. As we prayed, the peace of God permeated our hearts and we all had a sense that God was going to help us.

The one piece of good news from my doctor's appointment was that there is a treatment for the Hep C virus. It doesn't cure it, but it will bring it down to what they call the "undetectable stage" where it no longer damages your liver. That gives the liver an opportunity to begin to heal itself, but the treatment only works for 55% of the people. The way they know it is working is after you have been on the treatment for two months, your viral load should drop by 90%. Then every two months after that, it should drop by an additional 90%, until it can no longer be measured and is undetectable. For most people, it takes a year to get down to the undetectable stage, but because of the high viral load and the severity of the damage to my liver, if the treatment worked for me, I would have to stay on it for two years.

I started the treatment on March 20, 2006. Because of God's mercy and grace, the treatment began to work for me. Two months later in May, my viral load went from 10,600,000 to 787,000, dropping by more than 90%. In June it dropped to 43,000, again by more than 90%. Both my family and I were very encouraged, but the process was not easy. I guess no serious medical procedure is.

This treatment consists of a cocktail of two medicines. The first was a weekly injection of Interferon and the second was a daily dosage of two pills consisting of 600 milligrams of Ribavarin. I soon discovered medicines that help you in one way usually harm you in other ways. These are called side effects. There are other medicines you can take to combat these side effects, but initially, I resisted taking the other medicines because, in my thinking, it was absurd to take medicines to help me with the medicines.

One of the side effects I experienced from the weekly injection was sleeplessness. So after not sleeping for a month, I reluctantly starting to take a sleep medicine called Ambien CR. I was able to start sleeping, but the side effects of this medicine were memory lapses and disorientation. The side effects from the daily pills were loss of appetite and a metal taste in my mouth. The loss of appetite and metal taste caused me to lose over thirty pounds. The only medicine that would help me with this contains THC, which is the active ingredient in marijuana, so I refused to take that one and just tried dealing with weight loss by drinking a product called Ensure.

However, the most debilitating side effect I had to deal with was from the weekly injection. The doctors simply call this one "abnormal thinking." For someone who would never be accused of thinking normally in the first place, this took on a whole new meaning. I would take my injection on Monday morning, and for three days my mind would race, exaggerate circumstances, obsess over things, and cause extreme paranoia. Let me give you a few examples of what I'm talking about.

One day, I was sitting in my home office when I noticed the floors in the house needed cleaning. My wife was at her part-time job so she wasn't available to clean the floors. The more I stared at the dirt, the dirtier the house seemed to be. Finally, I decided to get up and vacuum the floors. While I was vacuuming the floors, I noticed other areas of the house that needed to be cleaned. Nine hours later, I had the entire house cleaned. When my wife got home, she tried to get me to stop, but I couldn't until all the dirt was gone. Though my wife was concerned about my obsession, she was pleased that she walked into a very clean house. Jokingly she asked me if I would mind if she rented me out to help the other women in the church with their housework.

My paranoia also became a problem. Since I couldn't travel and because the co-pay for the medicine was extremely high, our finances were really taking a hit. In July, our mortgage payment was two weeks late, but in my mind, I built it up to the point that I just knew we were going to lose everything. So I called up a realtor who went to our church and asked him if it was possible for me to sell my house by noon. He assured me it was not possible. I then called the bank that held our mortgage and told them to come get the keys to our house and for them to start the foreclosure process. Luckily, the loan person I talked with was an elder of the church I attend and he was able to talk me into waiting to see if things would change.

During this time, I twice tried to fire the board

members who oversee my ministry. I thought they didn't care about me and were out to destroy the ministry I had been serving for the last 22 years. The reason I tried firing them twice was because I didn't remember I had tried removing them a month earlier. I also experienced extreme agitation over anything and everything. I would snap at my wife and children over little things.

My outbursts of anger were really beginning to hurt my marriage and my family. These side effects would last until Wednesday night when that aspect of the medicine wore off. I would then regain my composure and my mental faculties. It got so bad that my pastor put a moratorium on me making any decisions between Monday and Wednesday. My wife would want to divorce me every Monday morning, but then she would want to remarry me every Wednesday night.

There was an anti-anxiety medicine I started taking for this called Lexipro. However, as more Interferon built up in my system, the less this medicine worked, until it quit working all together. The sickness and the medicine put a strain on every aspect of my life: my body; my mind; my emotions; my marriage; my family; my finances; and even my salvation. Nothing was left untouched, and everything I had, knew, and believed was being tested. This started me on a journey to understand why I got sick and how I could be healed.

THE TEACHING

For Christians, all journeys should start in Scripture. Psalm 119:105 states, "Thy word is a lamp to my feet, and a light to my path." I knew the answers to my questions and the provision for my problem would be found in the word of God. Psalm 107:19-20 clearly states, "Then they cried out to the LORD in their trouble; He saved them out of their distresses. He sent His word and healed them, and delivered them from their destructions." The *New Living Translation* says it this way, "LORD, help! They cried in their trouble, and He saved them from their distress. He spoke, and they were healed, snatched from the door of death."

This is what I needed, so I started searching the Bible for the words that would bring hope, faith, and ultimately healing to my body. I searched to see if there was anyone in the Bible who had experienced to any degree what I was. I found several, but the one who spoke to me the most was what the Apostle Paul went through in Asia Minor. He wrote about it in 2 Corinthians 1:8-11:

> For we do not want you to be unaware, brethren, of our affliction which came to us in Asia, that we were burdened excessively, beyond our strength, so that we despaired even of life; indeed, we had the sentence of death within ourselves in order that we should not trust in ourselves, but in God who raises the dead; who delivered us from so great a peril of death, and will deliver us, He on whom we have set our hope. And He will yet deliver us, you also joining in helping us through your prayers, that thanks may be given by many persons on our behalf for the favor bestowed upon us through the prayers of many.

I love the way *The Message* renders this passage,

> We don't want you in the dark, friends, about how hard it was when all this came down on us in Asia province. It was so bad we didn't think we were going to make it. We felt like we'd been sent to death row, that it was all over for us. As it turned out, it was the best thing that could have happened. Instead of trusting in our own strength or wits to get out of it, we were forced to trust God total-ly—not a bad idea since He's the God who raises the dead! And He did it, rescued us from certain doom. And He'll do it again, rescuing us as many times as we need rescuing. You and your prayers are part of the rescue operation—I don't want you in the dark about that either. I can see your faces even now, lifted in praise for God's deliverance of us, a rescue in which your prayers played such a crucial part.

The first thing that caught my eye as I began to med-itate on this passage was the link between prayers and the promise of deliverance. Paul knew and stated in verse 11 that "help and favor come through the many prayers of others." In *The Message* it reads this way: "that the prayers of others are part of the rescue operation." This encouraged me because over the years, I have prayed for thousands of people, many of them receiving a miracle to some degree, and now it was my turn to be on the receiving end of my prayers for myself. Surely the Lord would respond to my prayer for myself as He had responded to my prayers for others. In order to let God know how serious I was, I decided I would fast and pray for three weeks. I was confident that within those three weeks, I would be healed. At the end of three weeks, I had lost weight, but I didn't gain a healing. Though my body responded to the fast, the Lord didn't respond to my prayers.

I then thought if the Lord wouldn't respond to my prayer for me, maybe He would respond to the prayers of others for me. Therefore, I started asking everybody to pray for me. I told my cell group of my need and put it in both the monthly newsletter and the weekly e-letter I send out. When I ran into people who I didn't know at the gym, airports, or other places and found out in our conversations they were Christians, I would tell them of my need and ask them to pray for me. This was a little difficult because this sickness has some negative connotations to it. By asking people to pray for me, I was also letting them know something of my past sins and lifestyle. However, I couldn't afford to worry about that because I needed deliverance more than I needed dignity. But again, it didn't seem like God was responding.

I wasn't about to take no for an answer. If God wasn't going to respond to my prayers, maybe He would respond to His Word so I got a concordance and looked up all the passages I could find on healing. I compiled a list of them and divided that list by seven, so each day of the week I read and prayed one of those seven lists. Unfortunately, just as with the prayer and fasting, there still didn't seem to be any visible response from God.

At this point, I was both depressed and desperate, so I started staying up late at night and watching Trinity Broadcasting Network. I was hoping that one of the faith healers would miraculously call out my sickness on their broadcast and even if they asked me to put my hand on the TV and pray, I was prepared to do so. But as with everything else, nothing seemed to happen.

After all this, I went back to 2 Corinthians 1:8-11 to see if I missed anything since the "rescue" was not happening. This time, I saw a phrase in the passage that healing and deliverance are often not instantaneous, but a process. In the NASB, the phrase reads "in order that." *The Message* states it "as it turned out," indicating that even though the rescue didn't *immediately* happen, it did *ultimately* happen. It also indicated that God had a purpose for the problems Paul was experiencing, and that was to bring Paul to a place where he and his friends "no longer trusted in themselves but in God." Again, *The Message* interpretation is unique: "instead of trusting in our own strength or wits to get out of it, we were forced to trust God totally." Paul implied in this verse that once the purpose of "trusting in God totally" was accomplished, then deliverance from the problems followed.

As I meditated on this phrase, I sensed God speak to my heart these words: "Son, I know you are trusting Me for a healing, but will you trust Me with your health?" I interpreted this to mean that God was going to allow my health to be taken for a season in order to bring a much-needed seasoning to my life. As is my practice anytime I hear God speak by the still small voice, I then look to Scripture to see if what God has spoken resembles someone else's situation. I found several examples where this dynamic occurred. One of them was Job in the Old Testament and the other was Peter in the New Testament.

One of the things I began to understand is that the devil is God's devil. Psalm 119:91 states, "For all things are Thy servants." That being said, it stands to reason that Satan is God's servant. If you are a born-again believer in Jesus Christ, Satan has to get permission from God to do anything to you. We can see this in the Book of Job when Satan was given permission to afflict Job. We can also see this in Luke 22:31 where Satan asked permission of Jesus to sift Peter as wheat is sifted.

Everything the enemy does, God can use to serve His purpose. The weapons Satan uses to hurt us, God can use as tools to help us; the things he would use to tear us down, God can use to build us up; and the things he would use as stumbling blocks, God can use as steppingstones. In the afflicting of Job, God was glorified and Job was abundantly blessed. In the midst of being sifted, Peter had something transformed in him, which equipped him to be a strength to his brothers. Armed with understanding, I decided to stop trying to get out of my sickness and to allow God to use my sickness to get something out of me.

Since God wasn't going to deliver me from this affliction until I allowed Him to develop me through it, I started searching the Bible for some insight so I could learn my lessons well—and quickly. This search brought me to James 1:2-4 where in the *Phillips Translation* it states, "When all kinds of trials and temptations crowd into your lives, my brothers, don't resent them as intruders, but welcome them as friends." I began to see from this passage that God was trying to teach me that "trials" are part of His plan for my life, and the way I respond to them will either hinder or help this plan.

The first thing James pointed out about trials is that they come without invitation or permission, and begin to "crowd into my life." I may not like them, but I have to take the posture that I need them. If I see trials as "intruders," which is the way the enemy wants me to see them, then I will see them as being forced upon me to hurt me. As a result, I will spend all my time and energy trying to get them out of my life, instead of allowing them to get out of me those things that God is after. Therefore, I need to see them as "friends," sent by God to teach and transform me, as the rest of this passage in James attests: "Realize that they come to test your faith and produce in you the quality of endurance. But let the process go on until that endurance is fully developed, and you will find you have become men of mature character, men of integrity with no weak spots."

As I began to understand this, then instead of running from this fiery trial of physical sickness, I decided to remain in it until it yielded some treasure for my soul. And instead of praying "deliver me from" my present circumstances, I began to pray "develop me through." I also found that Paul in Philippians 4:10-12 had experienced the same understanding as James,

> But I rejoiced in the Lord greatly, that now at the last your care of me hath flourished again; wherein ye were also careful, but ye lacked opportunity. Not that I speak in respect of *want*: for I have learned, in whatsoever state I am, therewith to be *content*. I know both how to be abased, and I know how to abound: *everywhere and in all things I am instructed* both to be full and to be hungry, both to abound and to suffer need (KJV, emphasis added).

What makes Paul's statement both profound and powerful is where he was at when he wrote those words. He was in a Roman prison, shackled between two Praetorian guards. He wasn't seeing the opposition—imprisonment, shackles, loneliness—but rather the opportunity he then had to write the churches and to lead his guards to the Lord. His contentment came not from dwelling on what he didn't have, but realizing what he did have.

In verse 12, Paul gave us the secret to finding contentment in our present circumstances. He wrote, "everywhere and in all things I am instructed." The Greek word for *instructed* is *mueo*, which means *to initiate into the mysteries or knowledge of God*. The implication is that God has allowed my difficult situation in order to teach me something. In other words, until instruction took place, provision or deliverance would not.

I also found this same understanding in Psalms 46:1 which states, "God is our refuge and strength, a very present help in trouble." The question I had was, "Why didn't God help me out of the trouble?" I was beginning to understand that is not the order in which He does things. He must first adjust me to the trouble and cause me to learn my lesson from it. His promise is "I will be with you in trouble." He must be with me in the trouble first, before He would take me out of it. God used my present trouble to teach me some precious lessons. The trouble was intended to educate me.

From 1 Corinthians 10:13, I learned that when my faith is tested, I shouldn't look to escape the test, but to embrace it: "God is faithful, He will not let you be tested beyond more than you can stand. But when you are tested, He will also make a way out" (Beck). I like the rendering of this verse because the translator uses the word "test" instead of "temptation." If I saw the difficulty as a temptation, Satan would then try and use it to bring out the worst in me. If I saw it as a test, then God could use it to bring out the best in me.

The word temptation in the past caused me to misinterpret this verse, which then caused me to focus on the last part of the verse—"the way out"—instead of on the first part of the verse, "being able to stand." Paul was saying that the faithfulness of God would not let me be tested or tempted beyond what I was able to handle. It implies that if something is on me, then I can handle it, no matter what my feelings, friends, or finances say. If for some reason I buckle under the test, instead of standing in it, then God will provide "a way out." He does this because He will not let something He allowed into my life designed to help me begin to hurt me. Through this whole ordeal, I was learning that difficult experiences are designed to train and prepare me for a new movement of God's Spirit in my life.

I also discovered two stories in the Gospels which illustrate this principle. The first story is found in Mark 4:35-40 where Jesus told His disciples, "Let's go to the other side." As they got into the boat and launched out into the will of God, a furious storm (what I have come to see as standing operating procedure when we follow God) comes upon them. Even though most of these disciples were seasoned fishermen who have been in storms before, this storm was so bad that they began to fear for their lives. This fear caused them to wake the Lord, who was asleep (even though it was stormy), accusing Him of not caring about them. He got up, rebuked the storm, causing it to be still, and then He rebuked the disciples for having no faith.

This story is not about God's ability to still storms, but about God's ability to keep His disciples in the midst of storms. The stilling of the storm was a result of the disciples having no faith. It was not about Jesus' ability or intention to still the storm, but it was to set an example of how to get through the storm—which is by resting in it and not running from it. Jesus was trying to teach them through the storm that they had no reason to fear because He was in the boat with them. When He is in the boat with you, no storm can hurt you. By taking the way out, they didn't learn this lesson.

The second story is found in Matthew 14:22-32. This story is also about the Lord telling His disciples to "go to the other side," but as they do, another storm comes upon them. This time, Peter decided that he was going to be instructed by the storm instead of seeking deliverance from it. As a result, he learned to walk on the very thing (the water) that had previously threatened him. Jesus didn't still this storm, but once Peter passed the test, the storm was stilled instantly. Once he was instructed by it, he was then delivered from it. Through this, I learned that the best way to still a storm in my life is to be instructed by it.

Through this ten-month ordeal of having a life-threatening disease and as a result dealing with debilitating medicines, God educated, edified, and equipped me. Time and space will not allow me to tell you all the things God taught me during this time, but I do want to share with you two of the main ones.

The first is that God was after the indifference in my life toward people who were sick and on medicine. When I realized I was sick, I was 55 years old. All my life I had enjoyed good health. Because of this, I very rarely took any medication. Instead of being grateful to God for keeping sickness from me, I had the attitude I never got sick because I ate right and exercised daily. Because I believed my health was a result of something I did, I became indifferent and judgmental towards those who were sick.

Though I would try to act with compassion and care on the outside, my heart was callous and cold where their situation was concerned. I would pray for them if asked, but my prayers were ineffective because I prayed with no love and no faith. I had no love because I felt if they weren't so lazy and undisciplined, then they would be healthy and not need my prayers. I had no faith because I felt their sickness was God's judgment on their life because of the sins in the midst of their lives. When I heard that side effects of the medicine were affecting them emotionally and mentally, I thought they were using it as an excuse for bad behavior they didn't want to change.

As you might guess, I no longer feel that way. Though sickness is not from God, God used my sickness to deepen my capacity for compassion towards those who are sick because in the midst of all my right eating and disciplined exercise, I still got sick. I now realize that health is a blessing from God. I understand now the depths of despair, depression, and despondency that physical sickness can bring to a person. I understand now how important a caring look, a kind word, and a helping hand are to someone who has been robbed of their health.

But most of all, I understand the need for the kind of hope and faith that can only be imparted by someone who has walked in your shoes. Through this whole ordeal, it wasn't the healthy people who ministered the most to me, but those who had been or were still afflicted by some physical ailment. Their faith was able to touch me deep in my soul because it had been refined in the fires and storms of their own afflictions.

Through this, I learned you can't really comfort others in their afflictions until you have first been comforted in yours, which is clearly stated in 2 Corinthians 1:3-5: "The God of all comfort, who comforts us in all our affliction so that we will be able to comfort those who are in any affliction with the comfort with which we ourselves are comforted by God." Because I received compassion from so many, it imparted a much needed compassion for others in my soul. This compassion is actually allowing me to feel what others are feeling. It seems like I'm now able to feel the limp of the crippled; the hurt of the diseased; the loneliness of the outcast, and as an added bonus I'm now able to feel the embarrassment of the sinful. Once I feel their hurts, I'm compelled to do everything I can to heal their hurts. I have found that once I'm touched by their needs, I begin to forget my own. I'm learning that the best medicine for my problems is to get involved in someone else's.

The second thing God was after in my life was a weakened belief in the power of prayer. At the time I got sick, I had been a Christian for 33 years. In those 33 years, I had seen many tangible answers to prayers, but I was also aware of even more prayers going unanswered. In my early years as a Christian, I would pray about everything with an expectation that God would both hear and answer. But as the years went by, I began to pray less and less because more times than not, I felt like my prayers went unanswered.

Don't get me wrong, I still practiced the daily discipline of prayer in that I had daily devotionals. However, I did this more for the value of demonstrating to others that I had this discipline than I did in actually believing God heard or cared about my prayers. I still believed God answered prayers, but my weakened belief came from the perspective that He was selective in the prayers He chose to answer. Because I didn't know what qualified a prayer to be answered, I then stopped praying about most things, and the prayers I did pray were more a formality for the sake of others than an exercise of faith towards God.

Through this affliction, I learned that God responds to every prayer that is prayed. In 2 Corinthians 18-11, Paul understood that "help comes through the prayers of others." The word *help* in this passage means *to provide assistance*. It includes the notion of providing what is needed while you are still in the affliction so you may endure it until the lessons are learned. I'm so grateful for every prayer that was prayed on my behalf, for I realize now that without them, I would have perished in my affliction instead of persevering. God used those prayers to keep my marriage intact when the strain of the disease and the medicines were trying to tear it apart. God used those prayers to give my family and me enough hope to keep moving forward in the process, even when things seemed hopeless.

God used those prayers to move on people to assist us financially, when our personal finances were depleted. God used those prayers to move on people to call me or write me to lift me up, especially at the times I was at my lowest. God used those prayers to keep my board of directors loyal to me in the face of false accusations and the threat of being fired unjustly. The point I am trying to make is most of the prayers that were prayed on my behalf, God used to assist me while I was in the affliction, so that the lessons could be learned, which would then position me to be delivered from the affliction.

Also in 2 Corinthians 1:11, Paul made another statement about prayer: "God's favor is bestowed upon people through the prayers of many." The Greek word translated *favor* is *charisma* which is defined as *a gift of grace*. The implication is that once the assisting prayers have done their work and you have received the instruction you needed, He will then respond with favor by providing the gifts of grace you will need to be delivered. This brings me to the third and final part of this testimony.

THE TRIUMPH

By the end of August, I began to realize all the great things God had done in and for my life in the midst of this terrible affliction. As I became more compassionate toward the plights of others, I soon found myself praying for them with a faith I hadn't experienced since the early days of my Christian experience. I found myself thinking more of the sufferings of others than I was about myself. All this combined together gave me reasons to believe that soon God was going to bestow the "gift of grace" I would need to be delivered totally from this affliction.

I was encouraged because the medicine I was taking was working. My viral load over the previous eight months had dropped from 10,600,000 to 5,500. At that rate, soon I would be at what they call the "undetectable stage." As I mentioned earlier, at this stage the virus is no longer strong enough to do any more damage to my liver. Then because the liver is so resilient, it begins to heal itself. At this point, I was beginning to think the "gift of grace" God was going to use to deliver me was in the medicine I was taking.

All that hope came crashing down during my September visit to my doctor. I had hoped my viral load would have dropped by another 90%, but the opposite happened, it increased by 90% to 48,000. My doctor was convinced it was a lab error because it is rare for this medicine to begin to work and then stop. My doctor's assurance helped deal with our disappointment. They did some more tests, with the hope that when I came back a month later, it would verify my doctor's suspicion that it was a lab error. However, in October when I went for my visit, the tests showed that the medicine had indeed stopped working and my viral load was up to over 780,000 and still climbing.

At this point, I only had two options. The first, was to go on a daily injection of a much stronger medicine. If I chose this option, I would experience the side effects of abnormal thinking more intensely and would have no break from them since it was a daily instead of weekly injection. The doctor also told us that there was less than a 20% chance of this medicine even working. The other option was to wait for a new medicine that was coming out in two or three years that may help me. The problem with that option was my doctor didn't think I had two or three years left before my liver would fail and I would die.

Since the chances were that the first option wouldn't work anyway, Diane and I decided I should get an extensive liver biopsy, hoping it would show I had enough time left to wait for the new medicine. I left the doctor's office that day with a sense of hopelessness and despair. I was also disappointed and disillusioned because I felt I was learning the lessons God had been teaching me, and I had faith up until this point that the storm would soon be stilled.

During the next couple of days, I felt myself getting angry with God. Why had He abandoned me? Why did He give me hope only to take it away? When no answers came to these questions, I then resolved myself to the fact that I was probably going to die. At this point, my major concern was how my family was going to be provided for after I was gone. I had two children in college, a house mortgage, and car payments. I had no retirement, no life insurance, and no savings.

In the midst of my anger towards God, and my anxiety about my family, I felt my faith beginning to fail. Everything in me just wanted to give up. As I was sitting all stirred up with anger and anxiety, I was reading the story in Matthew 7 about the "wise and foolish builders." What caught my attention was that both the wise man and the foolish man had to endure a storm. The only difference between them was that the wise man's house stayed intact, whereas the foolish man's house was destroyed.

In that moment, I decided that even if this storm took my life, it was not going to take my faith. I resolved I was going to go through this storm with everything the Lord had given me intact. Not only was I not going to let the enemy rob from me, I was going to do everything I could to take back from him everything he had stolen from others. I was going to make him regret the day he had afflicted me. If I was going to die, I was going to die with gratitude in my heart, joy in my life, and a resolve to move forward in my faith. Just as the way I lived my life ministered to people, I now wanted the way I died to minister to them as well. I was determined that in these last few years, I was going to live my life in such a way that it would live on after I died.

Armed with this newfound resolve and the fact that I was no longer taking medicine, I began to travel and minister again. At the end of October of 2006, I was asked to conduct a weekend retreat for a church in St. Louis. The retreat was held at a retreat center about 100 miles south of the city. I had the privilege of ministering Saturday morning and evening and then again on Sunday morning. When I finished ministering on Sunday morning, I gave an altar call for people who wanted to be prayed for. The first people to come to the altar were the pastor of the church and his son, but instead of wanting me to pray for them, the pastor said they wanted to pray for me.

During the service, I had seen his eyes full of tears,

which I thought was the result of conviction over some sin. However, the tears he shed weren't over his sin but over my sickness. His son told me that God had given him a burden to pray for me. Before I go any further, I need to tell you a little about his son, Caleb. Though Caleb was the pastor's son, he wasn't known for his prayers, his Bible knowledge, his church attendance, or even his spiritual gifting. He was known as a good son who truly loved the Lord, but whose passions in life included being a fireman, hunting, and fishing. Therefore, I was a little surprised that of all the people in the church, God gave him a burden to pray for me.

I was even more surprised when he said that he simply wanted to pray the Lord's Prayer over me, and he even asked me if I would pray it with him. I must admit that I was touched by the fact he was burdened to the point of tears, and even though he wanted to pray for me, I didn't have any confidence that God was going to respond to this very simple prayer. When we prayed the part that says "Thy will be done on earth as it is in heaven," I sensed God touch me. At the time, I didn't think it was a healing touch, but more than anything, I felt the peace of God infuse my soul. I had the sense that no matter what happened, everything was going to be all right.

The following Tuesday was when my extensive liver biopsy was scheduled. The procedure went well and I was told my doctor should have the results by Friday. On Friday, I called my doctor and the secretary told me that he was out of town and wouldn't be back until the following Friday. I asked her if she could please call the doctor and ask him to give me a call back with the results from my biopsy. A little later, the secretary called me and told me the doctor had received the results, but he needed to discuss them with me face to face, and I would have to wait until the following Friday for that to happen.

This response from the doctor caused me to start thinking the worst. There is always a chance that cirrhosis of the liver can digress into cancer, but even with that possibility, I still sensed everything was going to be all right. I left on

Saturday to go minister at a church in Columbia, PA where I was to minister Sunday morning and then nightly through Wednesday night. While I was there, I was telling someone about my situation with the doctor, and they told me I didn't have to wait on the doctor, that I could get my own results from the medical records department at the hospital. I then called the hospital where my biopsy was performed and they verified what this person told me. Therefore, after the Wednesday night service I drove all night in order to get home by 7:00 a.m. A little while later, I drove to the hospital and had the records department make me a copy of all my test results.

As I stood in the hallway of the hospital reading my results, I could not believe what I was reading. The results revealed I had no steatosis, which meant I no longer had any fat in my liver. They revealed that there was no hepatocellular necrosis, which meant there was no longer any scarring on my liver. They revealed I no longer had a dangerous amount of iron in my liver, and in fact it was below normal. They revealed I no longer had a high amount of ammonia in my blood, and it too was in the normal range. And they revealed that I had no fibrosis, which meant that my liver damage was at "stage 0," indicating there was no damage at all.

As I was reading, I let out a yell of joy, a hospital employee walking by told me that I shouldn't yell in a hospital. I told them I had just found out that God had healed my liver and we both yelled with joy. I then went to where my wife worked in the hospital, shared the good news with her, and we rejoiced together. The next day, I went to my family doctor who is a Christian, and we both praised the Lord together. The following day, I went to the specialist who had been treating me, and I told him I had already received the results of my test. This doctor is not a Christian, and he told me that the reason he wanted to tell me the results face to face is that he couldn't explain them.

He proceeded to show me all the other test results indicating how bad my liver was, and how up until two weeks ago, I was not getting better but worse. I told him I could explain it, that God healed me. He couldn't believe that with me. He still believes that his original diagnosis was correct, and time will show that he was correct. He asked me to come back in six months for some more testing, which I agreed to do. The reason I agreed was that I want him to see that there is a God in heaven who is both all loving and all powerful.

It has now been 15 years since God healed me, and I feel better and stronger than I ever have in my life. I'm continuing to seek to learn from this ordeal. Luke 12:48 states, "Where much is given, much is required." Therefore, the more I can glean from this, the more I will be equipped to minister to others. As I stated earlier, I believe God responded to every prayer that was prayed on my behalf. All these prayers but one God used to provide me with grace that helped me to embrace my affliction while I was being educated by it. As I began to learn the lessons, then God responded to Caleb's prayer by providing for me His favor, a gift of grace, that then eradicated me from the affliction.

I believe God responded to Caleb's prayer because in responding to his prayer, God got all the glory. Caleb's prayer was a simple one, full of love for me and faith towards God. Caleb understood the power of prayer is not in the one who says it, but in the one who hears it. I'm grateful Caleb stepped into his fears, his lack of skill in prayer, and gave the little he had, hoping God could do a lot with it. And guess what? He did.

Caleb's prayer reminds me of the little boy who gave his sack lunch of two loaves and five fish to the disciples in order to feed a multitude of people as recorded in John 6:5-13. He only had a little, but he gave it in faith to a big God. The disciples attitude almost kept this miracle from happening because they said, "How far will they go among so many?" I believe this is the same attitude that keeps a lot of miracles from happening because most Christians only have a sack lunch, and because what they have won't go far, they won't let it go at all.

Through this whole ordeal, I have learned and am learning that God wants to do a whole lot more than we ever thought He would or could. The only thing he requires from us is the little we have, with the belief that in His hands, He can do a lot. I believe there are three parts to every miracle. There is the part of the one who is in need of a miracle—his or her part is to seek God for His purpose. There is the part of others who know and care for the one who needs a miracle—their part is to serve through their prayers. And there is God's part—which is to save through His power.

As I close out this testimony, I would like to share my appreciation for all the people who gave support to me and my family during this very difficult and debilitating time of my life. We felt this support at the church services where I ministered in the form of caring questions, encouraging words, and warm smiles. We felt this support through the continued financial support that sustained us and gave us faith to believe God would move on others as well. We also felt this support through the many prayers that were offered on our behalf during those very difficult days. I want to share my appreciation to God, and the best way I can show Him my appreciation is to allow Him to do through me what He has done for me.

Since then, I have shared this testimony many times all over the country and I have had the privilege of praying with others for them to receive their own miracle. The reason I have is not only because God has healed me, though that would be a sufficient reason, but because I can't *not* pray. Because of what I went through, I can no longer be indifferent toward the hurts of others, and I now realize more than ever how much power there is in prayer.

SUMMARY

This book contains some truths from God's Word that I discovered during some of the darkest times of my life. Not only did I pay a price to discover them as I sifted through the darkness to find the treasures that had the power to change and enrich my life, I also paid the price to apply them to my life and then also to release them from my life so they could enrich the lives of others.

Proverbs 23:23 states, "Buy truth and do not sell it." If you pay the price to live the truth, somewhere in that process the truth will pay you. You not only get in on the treasure, you also become a treasure for others. Before I go any farther, I want to make some disclaimers. I believe that Jesus dying on the cross and the shedding His blood for my sin paid the complete price for my salvation. This sacrifice not only removed our past but also secured our future. He did this all through His grace, which is unmerited favor. This grace not only gives me peace about my past, it also gives me faith for a prosperous future.

I won't go to heaven because I'm good, I'll go to heaven because Jesus was good for me. Martin Luther said, "The only thing we bring to the work of salvation is our sin." So, when I quote Proverbs 23:23, "Buy truth and do not sell it," I'm not talking about justification which has dealt with all our sin—past, present, and future. Nor am I talking about glorification which at the end of our lives enables our still "corruptible lives to put on His incorruption, and our mortality to put on His immortality" (1 Corinthians 15:53).

What I am talking about is sanctification a process through which the Spirit of truth guides us into the truth that will free us from our present sin as described in John 16:13: "When the Friend comes, the Spirit of the Truth, he will take you by the hand and guide you into all the truth there is" (MSG). I don't believe I will ever be completely sinless this side of glory, but because of His completed work on the cross, *positionally* I am sinless. What does that mean? It means I am clothed with the righteousness of Christ and thus I am in the position of being a completed work. If God where to paint a portrait of me, He would paint me without flaw because He is seeing me through the righteousness of Christ. However, experientiallyI still sin. Though I will never experience complete sin-lessness, through the sanctifying work of the Spirit of truth, I will sin less and less.

Also, temember that John 1:14 states, "Jesus was full of both grace and truth." His grace is granted for how we are but His truth is applied so we can become what we should. It is His grace that enables us to get back up after we sin, which has bound us, so we can keep moving towards His truth, which will free us. The currency enabling us to buy the truth that frees us is our obedience to that truth, along with our willingness to seek to apply the truth of God's Word to our lives.

Let me give you an example of how to "buy the truth." Proverbs 12:27 states, "A slothful man does not roast his prey, but the precious possession of a man is diligence." This hunter seeks his prey purely for sport. To him it is self-serving for he only wants trophy that he can display and about which he can brag. He is too lazy to skin, cut up, and then roast his prey, not only for his consumption where he would be nourished, but also for the consumption of others so they could be nourished. For some Christians, reading the Bible, listening to sermons, or reading Christian books are comparable to this hunter. They want to learn the truth so they can display it by sharing it with others, so others think they are spiritual. They never take the time to roast the truth by the painstaking effort to apply it to their lives (consuming it), where it is no longer just something they know, but has also become something they are—which changes them—and it becomes something they do—which changes others.

The last part of this passage talks about how "diligence is the precious possession of a man." Diligence is defined as *earnest and persistent application to an undertaking; steady effort; assiduity.* The *Amplified Bible* renders this part of the verse as "but the diligent man gets precious possessions." In other words, diligence in trying to apply God's truth to our lives is what will bring us all the precious possessions of this life, the "treasures hidden in darkness." That's why once you buy the truth, you will never sell it. I urge you to spend all you have to gain the treasures I have described in this book.

A WORD CONCERNING JIM NEWSOM

Jim Newsom is founder and executive director of Outward Focused International. Jim's life includes being expelled from high school, drug abuse, and criminal activity ranging from purse-snatching to armed robbery. Having been dishonorably discharged from the armed forces, Jim was ultimately charged and convicted of second-degree murder.

On July 26, 1972, Jim surrendered his life to Jesus Christ. The next morning, he turned himself into the local authorities, confessed to his crime and pled guilty to his charge. While in prison, he was instrumental in starting a prison church that is still in existence today. Having served eight years of a 30-year sentence, Jim was released in 1980. Since then, he has planted two churches and helped plant three more. He has also served as a youth minister, associate pastor and senior pastor in several churches.

In September 1983, a group of businessmen in Orlando, Florida asked Jim Newsom to relocate to their area to start a ministry that would minister to the least, the last and the lost. Since 1984, Outward Focused International has had a hand in establishing 5 churches, 5 prison ministries, and has helped train 14 men for full-time ministry.

Jim resides in Jeffersonville, Indiana with his wife, Diane.

CONTACT INFORMATION

Outward Focused International

3432 Christopher Trail

Jeffersonville, IN 47130

newsom035878@gmail.com

www.outwardfocusedinternational.net